'Adam Wordsworth writes a comprehensive exposé of the state-driven alienation of fathers from their children. While his initial motivation to write his book arose from his own experience of Family Court, he has successfully put passion aside and written a balanced and reasoned insight which argues the case for reform.

There are many nuggets in this book, such as the belief among politicians that there is a women's vote to be courted but not a men's vote, and that this has led to a bias in favour of women in legislation. He quotes Edmund Burke: "When leaders choose to make themselves bidders at an auction of popularity, their talents, in the construction of the state, will be no service."

This is a good and informative read.'

    - Ray Barry, Chair of Real Fathers for Justice.

The End of Discrimination:

What if U.K. family law was fairer?

Adam Wordsworth

Published in Great Britain in 2014 by
Springlands Press,
10 Broad Birches, Ellesmere Port, Cheshire, CH65 3AB
www.springlandspublishing.co.uk

A CIP catalogue record for this book is available from the
British Library.

ISBN 978-0-9929733-0-8

Adam Wordsworth is a graduate of Social Sciences & Politics from the Open University. He lives in Cheshire with his partner and daughters (sometimes). This is his first publication.

For my daughter, Isabel,
without whom I would never have
given this issue a second thought.

Contents

Index of Abbreviations

CIPD
Chartered Institute of Personnel & Development; Human
Resources professional body

CSA
Child Support Agency; institution charged with regulating,
collecting and enforcing child support payments

CMEC
Child Maintenance and Enforcement Commission

CTC
Child Tax Credit; benefits payable to lower income workers
for each child in their care

DWP
Department of Work and Pensions

ECHR
European Convention of Human Rights; international treaty to
protect human rights. Entered into force 3rd September, 1953

F4J
Fathers 4 Justice; campaign organisation for fathers' rights

FJR
Family Justice Review; panel created to scrutinise most areas
of family law, reported their findings in November 2011

HRA

Human Rights Act 1998

JSA

Jobseekers Allowance; benefit payable to those actively seeking employment

MP

Member of Parliament

PM

The Prime Minister

PMQ

Prime Minister's Questions; House of Commons event whereby the Leader of the Opposition and other MPs may challenge the Prime Minister of the day on issues of government

RSA

Royal Society for the encouragement of Arts, Manufacturing and Commerce; U.K. think tank

SSCBA

Social Security Contributions and Benefits Act 1992

TCA

The Children Act 1989

TCSA

The Child Support Act 1991

TUC
Trade Union Congress

WTC
Working Tax Credit; benefit payable to lower income workers

Foreword

Who should read this?

Everyone, be they taxpayer, parent, Social Worker, Politician, anyone with a social conscience and a desire for our country to provide for, and better protect, our children. I'll include Family Court Judges, Family law Solicitors and any other Family Law expert for though they will be aware of the shortcomings of the system they should welcome a different perspective on their current practices, or will they?

I fought UK Family Law for 11 years. All I initially wanted was contact with my son and then for the contact to be upheld. I gave up on Solicitors and blundered my way through the Family Court process believing that someone somewhere would uphold the right of my son to have a full and proper relationship with his entire family. It was bewildering and heartbreaking. This book shows an alternative to the madness and the emotional turmoil warring parents can put their children through.

Additionally this body of work both addresses the current Child Support system and explores issues which I wish I had understood many years ago. While I was fighting the Family Court process I was also wrestling with an unbelievably incompetent and needlessly belligerent Child Support Agency. Here Adam Wordsworth again explores the alternatives and offers constructive and viable argument for reform.

Acquiring a Court Order for contact with your child can be a lengthy, expensive and traumatic experience and no-one tells you that unlike the many bank notes you will be required to exchange to obtain it, the order carries no promises. Neither is there any recourse for a vindictive parent with care who is willing to commit multiple counts of perjury and/or defy countless Court Orders for contact. With the current system, while fighting through the court precious time is passing, and in a case of Implacable Hostility it becomes easy for a parent with care to knowingly (or unwittingly) alienate the absent parent. Once it can be demonstrated that contact will be too distressing for the child, contact will not be ordered. Herein lays the loophole, the license, the incentive for a vindictive parent with care to emotionally abuse the child. To quote Karen Woodall "Where there is Implacable Hostility there is a personality disorder". Such an environment is toxic to a child's development it is abuse that will not heal so easy as a bruise or a broken limb, yet is incredibly more difficult to prove or get anyone to take note and act upon. Again, Wordsworth shows a way to pre-empt such wicked manipulation of both the child(ren) and the structure we entrust them to with a duty of care.

Adam Wordsworth is to 21st Century Children & their families what James Brown was to Rock & Roll going beyond contemporary boundaries, identifying and seeking excellence in opportunities beyond the traditional rhythm. He puts into clear English every common sense issue I was fighting. He explains the evolution of the current Family law system and the desperate need for change. Peeling back layer by layer and addressing how we fail our children currently and how simple the alternatives are. Wordsworth acknowledges the complexities of engaging Political influence and delves into why Family law reform and equal parenting principles are often seen as an affront to feminists and an issue that risks political suicide if upsetting the female voter. He then takes the starting point of equal parenting analysing it from every angle and demonstrating that far from this being gender biased it is actually in the best interest of the child(ren) on a multiple of levels AND a recognition of male/female equality.

It does not have to be 50/50 as the majority of parents will fine tune and agree a parenting plan to best suit their individual situation. But 50/50 should be the default starting point. (Read on and all will be explained)…

Thomas Moore
Author of Please…Let Me See My Son

i. Preface

Sitting in a courtroom at Chester's Family Court in June 2011 ready to argue my case I saw the situation very clearly. I had clarified my argument and was certain about the reasonableness of my position. The judge saw the situation very clearly as well, but in stark contrast to my own point of view. And he had no compunction about voicing this opinion during the hearing, much to my embarrassment.

So was I wrong? Well the short answer is yes. The long answer: maybe. In terms of the way the law stands I could not have been further removed. The idea of requesting to see my daughter for half of the time without the consent of her mother is simply unacceptable under current U.K. family law (the idea of having full custody was never even up for discussion). So in this sense, yes, I was wrong. In terms of doing what is right by the parents and by the child, the issue is not so clear cut. In fact it is a polarising issue and the two schools of thought may well be irreconcilable. On the one hand there are sects that argue that the best interests of a child whose parents are separated are to be with the mother, or at least with one parent, rather than split between two. The other school of thought argues that a child is better served by having two parents as fully involved as they can be.

Had I written this book in the immediate aftermath of that court hearing in 2011, it would undoubtedly have been a 30,000 word angry diatribe directed at the family justice system. That is not, however, what I did. I left the court, accepted the judgment and started to research the substance of family law so as better to understand what had happened to my family and why.

Two years later it became apparent that there are impassioned arguments both for and against reforming that system, and my desire to document these became the inspiration for this book. These two years have involved a lot of work and a lot of commitment, not just in terms of time, and as with any project, to use the old cliché, I couldn't have done it alone. I would like to thank my partner, Victoria, for tolerating the moodiness (and neglect!) that invariably ensues whenever I have a project that I get my teeth into. Thanks also to my parents for their love and support in everything I do.

To my brother, Tom, both for organising my paperwork in 2011 and for doing more than his share of the legwork in 2013. Also considerable thanks to Colin Davies and Paul Magee. I am sure that they don't ascribe to many of the arguments expressed within these pages, but their understanding of the law in this area is exceptional and I couldn't have developed this volume, or an appreciation of why the law is what it is, without their insights.

There is little evidence to suggest that the law is going to change in the near future, so in that sense the following remains hypothetical. That said, it doesn't mean that it is not worth striving for or indeed writing about. In the words of a certain aspiring U.S. Presidential candidate in 2009, "change will not come if we wait for some other person or some other time. We are the ones we've been waiting for. We are the change we seek."

Adam Wordsworth, July 2014

ii. Prologue

It was regarding a matter completely unrelated to anything relevant to this book that the Bar Council (which represents barristers in England and Wales) published a report in June 2013. Many of the assertions therein were generalisations lauded by the public and the press alike as accurate and evidence to support the agenda of the report itself. That report was related to the government's proposed changes to legal aid and access to it, but in order to pull support for its opposition to those proposals, the Bar Council argued the merits of the current system; not just the current means of distributing legal aid but the current justice system in its entirety, for this was surely a model that should be emulated the world over. In the report they claimed that *"the British justice system... is renowned worldwide for fairness and impartiality."*[1] This is clearly a bold statement but also a plausible one. Law in the UK is drawn up by directly elected representatives of the people, so it should be safe to assume that laws reflect the views of society, or certainly the views of the electorate. Given that these laws, made on behalf of the people and reflecting their beliefs, are then administered 'fairly' and 'impartially', in the words of the Bar Council, there can surely be little cause for contention and little reason for people to dispute rulings or argue that the rules are unjust or that the administration of the rules is discriminatory.

However, there is an area of law in which arguments such as these are being made with increasing frequency and vigour. Certain groups claim that in family law, not only are the rules unfair, but, contrary to being *impartial*, they are necessarily *partial*. Clearly these two viewpoints are diametrically opposed and so the question becomes *which one is accurate?*

All aspects of the delivery of justice necessitate contention, whether that contention is between victim and defendant in criminal law, claimant and defendant in civil law or between two separated parties in family law. This last area, however, is arguably emotionally the most highly charged as the decisions made therein can impact upon every aspect of each party's lives, and the lives of their dependants.

In November 2011 news broke that the Family Justice Review (FJR) – a committee established to consider possible widespread changes to family law and the administration of family law – was to submit its final report stating that there were to be no recommended changes in one of the most contentious areas: that of child custody in the event of parental separation. The report stated that:

*"The child's welfare should be the court's paramount consideration, as required by the Children Act 1989. No change should be made that might compromise this principle. Accordingly, **no legislation should be introduced that creates or risks creating the perception that there is a parental right to substantially shared or equal time for both parents.*** For that reason and taking account of further evidence we also do not recommend a change canvassed in our interim report that legislation might state the importance to the child of a meaningful relationship with both parents after their separation where this is safe. While true, and indeed a principle that guides court decisions, we have concluded that this would do more harm than good".*[2]

*my highlights

This decision caused controversy amongst campaigners for fathers' rights, who believed that The Children Act and subsequent rulings by the family courts have consistently favoured the mother in cases of separation and that the father is treated as a second-class parent. In discovering the news of the contents of the FJR report Nadine O'Connor, Campaign Director for Fathers 4 Justice, said "this whole exercise has been designed to appease women's groups, not fathers."[3] This comment made the suggestion, not for the first time, that law-making is not necessarily about fairness, but is a political process and decisions are affected by political calculations.

Fathers 4 Justice itself is a campaign organisation founded in 2001 by Matt O'Connor, a man who went through the court process trying to gain access to his sons. They gained much publicity by dressing up as superheroes to protest at high profile buildings and once threw coloured flour at the then Prime Minister Tony Blair during Prime Minister's Questions (the famous 'Fun Powder Plot'). People often go to these lengths because they feel driven to by what they see as the injustices in the current system of family law. Many fathers who go through the custody process would argue that because they make up 50% of their children's parents, gaining access every other weekend (15% of the time) isn't acceptable, and so equal rights as a parent in the eyes of the law should be the very first change made.

The title of this book is in itself controversial and deliberately so: *The End of Discrimination* suggests the presence of discrimination to begin with. Whether people adhere to the view that changes to family law to give fathers equal rights to mothers are needed or it is, as the FJR claims, more likely to do harm than good, it would be difficult to find someone who would argue that the delivery of justice in this area is *not* prejudiced, because it is designed to be so. This book has not been written as a campaign either for changes to- or maintenance of the status quo, rather a consideration of what the consequences – both intentional and otherwise – of giving both parents similar standings in custody disputes would be.

It will look at the successive pieces of legislation that have together made the landscape of family law what it is today before going on to consider the effects that the above changes would have, if implemented, on the courts that administer the law, on women in general and mothers in particular, on industry, on the benefits system, on agencies such as the CSA and most importantly, on the children involved. It will consider the political effects and the reasons why successive governments have chosen to maintain the status quo. In other words, was the FJR correct in saying that equal parenting would do more harm than good? Would the creation of equal parenting rights lead to the end of society as we know it, or to the end of the last acceptable form of discrimination?

A Piecemeal Approach

The current state of affairs and proposed changes

"All mothers and most fathers have legal rights and responsibilities as a parent – known as 'parental responsibility'"

- www.gov.uk; the U.K. government information website, August 2013

You could be forgiven for taking exception to the above quote, written on the official website of the U.K. government under the link 'what is parental responsibility?' It could be conceived many people might have a problem with this whereas others might think it is a perfectly acceptable statement. If you don't see what all the fuss is about then don't worry; we will be returning to it later. Firstly, though, a comprehensive assessment of whether or not the law needs to be reformed cannot be undertaken without an overview of the current laws and their implications.

The law today regarding child custody largely traces its roots back to 1989 and The Children Act (TCA) passed that year (although there have been subsequent pieces of legislation passed, The Children Act is still the main authority in terms of rules governing this area of law and any more recent reviews of legislation have always worked within the spirit of this statute). Proponents of the status quo would argue that TCA does not in itself discriminate against anybody and that statistics presented by fathers' groups to illustrate that the law is applied in a prejudicial manner are simply a reflection of the circumstances of particular families which happen to be reflective of the make-up of society as a whole. Again this will be explained and evaluated in more detail later. The 'spirit' of TCA that has been mentioned was summed up in Section 1 of the Act, as if to anticipate the arguments that would surely otherwise ensue in Sections 2 - 108. It states:

"When a court determines any question with respect to –
> *(a) the upbringing of a child; or*
> *(b) the administration of a child's property or the application of income arising from it,*

the child's welfare shall be the court's paramount consideration *"*[4]

That the child's welfare shall be the court's paramount consideration has become known as the "paramountcy principle" or the "welfare principle" and all legislation developed in this area has paid consideration to it. As a point of principle this seems a reasonable premise on which to build an Act aimed at the protection of children.

Supporters of the status quo are clear that the situation as it stands focuses on the welfare of the child, rather than the rights of the parents, and so it should. It is not the fault of the child that two parents cannot agree a custody arrangement and therefore a pragmatic approach of one parent gaining full residence, for example, is more beneficial to the child (as it involves far less time arguing in court) than something a little less clear cut. They would further argue that there is no court bias against fathers and no gender bias written into legislation. In fact when this issue was brought against the family courts nearly a decade ago Dame Elizabeth Butler Sloss – a court judge, then head of the Family Division – told the constitutional affairs committee hearing into the family court system that there was no bias against fathers and that *"there is nothing in the law to lead courts to choose one parent or another."*[5]

So was Dame Butler Sloss correct? John Baker, then Chair of the campaign group Families Need Fathers wrote a press release in 2004 in response to Dame Butler Sloss' testimony claiming that she was *"profoundly mistaken"*. He alleged that the family justice system was *"institutionally sexist"* but went on to acknowledge that

"The formal law...states that the welfare of the children is the first and paramount consideration, and does not require that this be interpreted in a sexist way"[6]

Here Baker seems to accept Dame Butler Sloss' premise *that "there is nothing in the law"* to suggest a gender bias should be applied, but he places the blame entirely in the hands of the courts for the law being *"interpreted in a sexist way"* in that they decide that the children are *"best off if their mother, by virtue of her sex, is put in charge"*. Baker's repost was forceful and emotive, but it is another fathers' campaign group – Fathers 4 Justice – who provide the empirical evidence that seems to support Baker's argument that there is a systemic skew against fathers in the family courts. All the following statistics were sourced directly from Fathers 4 Justice (www.fathers-4-justic.org, 2013):

1 in 3 children live without their father in the U.K, amounting to 3.8 million children in total. This is not to say that 1 in 3 *children of divorce* live without their father but when considering the volume of couples still together where the children live with both parents, this suggests a large number of residency orders being awarded in favour of the mother, rather than the father.

27.6% of children live with their mother [alone], just 2.4% live with their father [alone] as of 2007. This links in with the next statistic that:

93.1% of broken families are headed by a single mother.

These statistics paint the picture of a system that believes, rightly or wrongly, that children do not belong with single fathers. Families Need Fathers clearly believe that the courts are institutionally biased against fathers, but this does not address the premise raised by Dame Butler Sloss that there is nothing "in the law" to lead a court to side with one parent over another. Again we must consider the evidence. Is there in fact nothing written into legislation that gives one parent – mother or father – preference over the other in cases of family law? This is the point at which we return to the quote at the start of the chapter. This quote refers directly to TCA which defines parental responsibility (Section 3) and determines who automatically has it (Section 2). Under Section 2 of TCA a mother automatically has parental responsibility for her child but a father does not necessarily (unless he is married to the mother). In fact, Section 2(4) states clearly, as if to reinforce the position that this rule was not an oversight or error in drafting, that *the rule of law that a father is the natural guardian of his legitimate child is abolished*. As a further affront to fathers, Section 4 of that same Act lists the ways in which a father may go about acquiring parental responsibility for his child, if he so wishes (for example, by making an agreement with the mother [Section 4(1)(b)] or by making an application to the court [Section 4(1)(c)]). It seems that TCA, seen in itself as the cornerstone of family law in the U.K., does contain gender biases.

The next piece of legislation to be considered is the Social Security Contributions and Benefits Act 1992 (SSCBA). Schedule 10 of this bill deals with *Priority Between Persons Entitled To Child Benefit* and paragraph 3 states that where a husband and wife are living together, the wife shall be entitled to the benefit, whereas paragraph 4 states that where two unmarried parents are together the mother shall be entitled to the benefit. Again, it is hardly life altering given that it addresses situations in which the parents are still together but it is certainly a direct gender bias, albeit possibly written for reasons of pragmatism (Why trouble the courts with something as tedious as a married couple squabbling over which one of them should receive state support when in one sentence the argument can be settled?). It is not too difficult to imagine, though, in some instances whereby a family has broken down and the parents are fighting over custody of the child, that a judge may be swayed to award custody to the parent receiving the child benefit, as they may be seen as the primary carer as a result. If this parent is necessarily the mother, this may, hypothetically, cause a gender prejudice.

Finally there is The Child Support Act 1991 (TCSA). This piece of legislation labels the non-resident parent as the *"absent parent"* and Section 1 states that *"it shall be the duty of the absent parent"* to make periodical payments of child support. Given the statistics considered above we can safely assume that the "absent parent" in the vast majority of cases, for whatever reason, means "the father". That being the case what this all means is that the father must make periodical payments to the mother. An "absent parent" will pay more in child support the more they earn and they will also pay more the less they see their child (the idea being that they are contributing to the food, clothing etc. for the child whilst the child is not in their care). However, it is the labels "resident parent" and "absent parent" (which are applied in every case) that determine who pays whom, not how much time a child spends with each parent. In other words if a father is classified as the "absent parent", even if he has the child live with him exactly 50% of the time (so he will be paying for food, clothing etc. half the time, the mother paying the other half), he will still be obligated to make a child support payment to the mother (an "absent parent" on a £30,000 per annum salary would be expected to pay £23 per week if the child splits their time equally between the two parents). This anomaly has led fathers' groups to label child support as a 'tax on fatherhood'.

These pieces of legislation do seem to contradict Dame Butler Sloss' claims that there is no legal basis for prejudice in family law. These laws in themselves may not force a court's hand in choosing "one parent over another", but they are surely indicative of the intentions of those drafting the law (which judges are bound to take into account) and it is often argued by fathers' groups that several of these 'little' laws combine to create an overwhelming tide against which fathers must swim to get through a legal battle with a mother.

What, though, is the alternative? John Baker, in the response he wrote for Elizabeth Butler Sloss argued that the law should be amended to accommodate the following:

"1) Both parents being given residence orders unless there are contra-indications. Both having residence orders does not determine the allocation of the children's time with each

parent. However, it places them in a position of joint formal and symbolic authority. The number of shared residence orders is increasing, in part as a result of Dame Elizabeth having lowered the barriers to the award of them. They remain a small minority of orders. Most still polarise the parents into winners and losers of residence orders.

2) The starting point of discussions of parenting time being equality. There may well be departures from it in most cases for necessary child-centred and practical reasons. But departures from it should be the ones that require justification. At present the assumption is that one parent has possession and the other has to argue that the children should be 'allowed' time with them.

3) More equality of parenting time. Fathers now provide one third of childcare in intact families. In the event of family division and a failure of the parents to agree the normal order of parenting time still revolves around a fortnightly stay, a visit in the week and some holiday time, all subject to the approval of the mother. Loved and loving children and parents may lose two-thirds of their time together; more if there is continuing ill-feeling between the parents. In many cases the children may suffer a permanent loss of contact with their non-residential parent.

4) Enforcement of court orders. There is some movement towards courts insisting that the children actually get the parenting time ordered. Enforcement remains extremely patchy. The perception of residential parents - that they can still do what they want - is broadly accurate.

5) Non residential parents can be excluded from the lives of their children without sufficient reason, for example by unproven allegations of domestic violence or abuse. Allegations should be investigated even-handedly and action should be taken against claims which are false or malicious.

Above all the law and society still condones the notion that when parents break up the children are now part of a 'one parent' family. The other parent has many barriers to overcome - financial, practical, legal, housing, emotional - to retain and develop an involvement with the children. There should be a formal legal presumption that children are entitled to a full and free relationship with both their parents, unless sufficient cause is shown that this would be against their welfare."

Points 1-3 here relate to shared parenting arrangements and there are many arguments for and against this becoming standard policy. When fathers' groups advocate the need for shared parenting on the basis that the current system is weighted against them, defenders of the current system will maintain that the law is designed, in the spirit of TCA, to look after the interests of the children, not to protect the rights of the parents. Therefore even if the system is prejudicial, this is meaningless because it is not the parents who it is trying to protect. With that in mind the main argument against shared parenting is the issue of stability for the child. The argument goes that if one parent doesn't have the sole authority to make decisions relating to a child's needs such as schooling, activities etc (Baker's point 1) and if a child is to spend time between two homes (Baker's point 2) then they will never understand where they belong, where home is or who makes the decisions affecting them. The consequences of this could be that they end up confused and this confusion in the younger years may manifest itself in other ways in later years – anger, poor social skills, criminality.

The counter argument here is that children living within the traditional nuclear family also move between a number of child care environments and they also see a number of adult decision-makers in their lives that they are expected to treat with respect. Children in these families may be cared for by one parent during the day, another during the evening or doing the school run. They go to school and are cared for by teachers, minded by grandparents and left in the care of organisers of activities. In these instances nobody challenges the destabilising effect of these routines and, in fact, it can be argued that as long as a child knows in advance where they are going, what they will be doing and with whom, these routines provide stability in themselves.

A further argument is that the award of a joint custody agreement may well cause ongoing conflict between the parents whereas sole custody ends conflict there and then. This seems rather simplistic and, again, looking at the nuclear family there are often disagreements between parents who are still together over issues such as parenting techniques and decisions made about the child. This is never challenged as destabilising.

None of these arguments, though, address the theme of this book which is the consideration of equality in the law. That is, shared residence with a 50/50 split of time would surely be 'fair' to both parents, but as we have seen there are arguments against. That doesn't mean that the law has to be weighted towards one parent (as quoted above, 93% of single parent families are headed by a single mother). Jon Elster, wrote a book entitled 'Solomonic Judgments; Against The Best Interests Of The Child' (the title referring to a custody dispute put before King Solomon of Israel in which the child was given to his mother. Albeit this dispute was between two women both claiming to be the real mother of the child this title at least suggests that, if true, custody arguments have been raging for at least the last 3,000 years so I make no apologies if I am unable to settle the matter in 2014!). In his book Elster argued for shared parenting but went on to make the point, only somewhat tongue-in-cheek, that if the state is determined to allocate sole residence to one parent then there is no reason not to make the decision based on the flip of a coin.[7] This would at least have the dual effect of silencing the advocates of sole custody whilst being indisputably impartial.

Baker's fourth point refers to the enforcement of court orders, which is an area fraught with difficulty. As a lawyer I spoke with recently put it:

"In my experience mothers regard parental responsibility as something to be given lip service rather than to be promoted. They will give the father little or no consultation regarding education or medical treatment. Orders from the court can say something has to happen but that does not necessarily then happen in practice. A father is told he is equal and has parental responsibility but how does he enforce that? A court will say that a father is equal but then in practice it falls on the mother to comply."

This idea makes little sense to the layperson who may consider that an order directed by a court is something sovereign, which cannot be breached. Surely there are means of enforcing any order given by any court in the land? Said the same lawyer:

"There are court sanctions that can be imposed on a mother who refuses to comply with an order. A court can, for example, change a residence agreement. I have never found a judge prepared to send a mother to prison (although it can happen) but they can change residence arrangements."

At this point in the conversation I was leaning to the idea that the matter was settled. A court will impose an order, a parent will comply with that order or else a judge may send them to prison, or more likely give residence to the other parent. This must mean that Baker is mistaken. However, when discussing the issue of enforcement in more detail, this lawyer conceded that this is a weakness in the family law system:

"[Assume that] a person says that a parent is being unreasonable. A court will often give that parent the benefit of the doubt for the first few occasions until it becomes a recurring problem. Where there is a clear pattern of this sort of behaviour a judge will use something such as a fine, imprisonment or the threat of imprisonment. If the behaviour improves, say, and then a few months down the line it again slips, it is extremely rare for a judge to send someone to prison as he has to consider the impact this has on the children. And how would the children view the parent that they see as responsible for sending the other one to prison? A more likely outcome is that residence switches. [But] As a judge I need to balance the swapping of the order with the interests of the child. [So] This is also rare as it affects a

child's entire life. So the process usually involves many court hearings over a long period of time during which fathers get frustrated and often give up, whereas mothers get buoyed by a court's lack of action."

So the ability to enforce is there, but the paramountcy principle, which is the driving force behind the belief that a child should reside solely with one parent, is also the principle that makes a court loathe to enforce its own orders. The fact is that these principles were clearly made with good intentions and they are sound; a child's welfare should be the first consideration. The only question really is whether a child is better off with one stable home or with two involved parents.

For the sake of argument we shall consider Baker's 5 point plan as the blueprint for change so the next consideration must be what effects these changes would have in practice; whether they are feasible and whether they are beneficial to all concerned, particularly the children

Pragmatism or Justice?
Effects of changes on the Family Courts

"The [family justice system] is, first and foremost, a justice system"

- Lord Phillips and Lady Hale, 2011[8]

Justice is a difficult concept to define. When asked what justice is, the first words that usually spring to people's minds are 'fairness', 'reasonableness', 'equality'. These terms in themselves, though, are complex and contested and it is not even universally accepted that any of them should play a part in a definition of justice. Lord Wright commented on the difficulty in finding an acceptable definition when he said:

"the guiding principle of a judge in deciding cases is to do justice; that is justice according to the law, but still justice. I have not found any satisfactory definition of justice…what is just in a particular case is what appears to be just to the just man, in the same way as what is reasonable appears to be reasonable to the reasonable man"[9]

Knowing that he wants to do justice without knowing exactly what that means doesn't inspire a great deal of confidence. That is to say that if justice is subjective then it will rarely be realised. Some (mainly literalist lawyers) claim that the rigid application of rules without accounting for particular circumstances creates certainty and, thereby, fairness. This in itself is justice.

It could be argued, though, that rulings made in a consistent manner without consideration for the substance of the case before the court or without consideration of the fairness of the rules in the first place, is not necessarily just. For example, if the law was rewritten legalising murder and, subsequently, the courts ruled in every case brought before them that intentionally killing another human being is not an offence, then the law could be said to have been applied consistently in every case. But is this fair or indeed just?

A working definition for justice can be brought to us by every social scientist's favourite philosopher; John Rawls. Rawls wrote *A Theory of Justice* in 1972 which was effectively a criticism of the inequities which would be implemented should entirely utilitarian laws be enacted. He strongly urged that 'the greater good' was no excuse for blatant injustice. He started with a basic premise in stating that justice is effectively about equality. *"The meaning of equality"*, Rawls claimed, *"is specified by the principles of justice which require that equal basic rights be assigned to all persons."*[10] This seems a fairly obvious position to take; equality is the counter to inequality, and nobody wants *that*. In order further to define justice he explained that *"the principles of justice I shall call justice as fairness."*[11]

It is arduous work picking through Rawls' lengthy thesis but in summary he argued that people – you and I, in effect – should envisage ourselves in what he termed 'the original position' and then decide what laws we would draw up together to regulate our lives. The original position is an imaginary place completely removed from society in which nobody knows anything about what their identity will be *inside* society, thereby they cannot be guided by their individual prejudices and therefore whatever rules they draw up should be fair. People in the original position are behind what Rawls referred to as a 'veil of ignorance'; they know nothing about their age, class, gender, religion etc. Ben Rogers explained the theory in a delightful critique almost three decades after the original work was published, in which he stated that:

"society is, of course, involuntary, and our place in it largely beyond our control, but Rawls asks what arrangements people would consent to if it were *freely entered into, and then tries to construct society on that basis"*[12]

The reason for the necessity of the veil of ignorance needs little explanation: if we knew who we were then we would likely draw up laws that would be to our benefit. Just laws, then, are ones which can be said that all individuals would establish for the whole of society if they knew nothing about themselves beforehand. Rawls claimed that people in the original position would take a low risk approach to rule making, so they would probably create rules that would not inflict suffering upon themselves, regardless of who they are (in other words they would rather, for example, create rules safeguarding against being poor at the expense of the rich, than allowing more people to become wealthy with the cost of higher poverty).

Now it must be considered whether the current situation in family law means that a judge is able, in the words of Lord Wright, to *"do justice"*. Assuming that Rawls' definition of justice is, if not perfect, about right, the law should be measured against his two basic principles:

1. Justice as fairness in that *equal basic rights be assigned to all persons* and

2. People in the *original position* would consent to being subject to these laws

In consideration of the first principle, as was shown in the last chapter there is little equality in family law. Again, this is deliberately so and many would argue that the current system is the only one that can work, but for a consideration of justice led by equality, the status quo certainly seems to stray from this principle. As already stated the law in several areas gives preference to mothers over fathers (Section 2/3/4 TCA, Schedule 10 SSCBA, Section 1 TCSA, see chapter 1) and the courts tend to give preference to mothers over fathers (see statistics on single parent families, chapter 1). So equal rights are not assigned to all persons and certainly not to all parents.

In consideration of the second principle, in order to establish whether or not the present situation would be acceptable it is necessary to imagine ourselves in the original position, which is, admittedly, a difficult thing to do. Bearing in mind that people behind the veil of ignorance would have no concept of who they are when living in society, those drawing up laws would not know their own gender, and therefore which side of the divide they would be on should they be unfortunate enough to experience a family breakdown. In that situation it is difficult to imagine anybody consenting to a law that states that in the event of a separation involving children there is a 50% chance that they would be forced to lose contact with their children (but for minimal access every-other weekend). If Rawls was correct about people taking a low risk approach to law making, then they would surely find a way to treat parents equally thereby allowing them all time with their children, and consequently acknowledging a child's right to have a relationship with both parents.

There must be other principles involved, though, in the creation and administration of law, than simply doing justice. As mentioned in the prologue, the FJR considered shared parenting when laying out its proposals for the future of family law in 2011. During this it commented that *"no legislation should be introduced that creates or risks creating the perception that there is a parental right to substantially shared or equal time for both parents...we also do not recommend a change canvassed in our interim report that legislation might state the importance to the child of a meaningful relationship with both parents after their separation...we have concluded that this would do more harm than good"*.

What the FJR meant by *"more harm than good"* was that it would be difficult to define a 'meaningful relationship', may cause an extra strain on the courts and would be difficult to enforce. Indeed they justified the removal of a recommendation for a parent to have a 'meaningful relationship' with their child as a right because it would make matters too complicated:

"Rather than introducing a provision that creates problems and then adding a fix to those problems, it would be far more sensible not to introduce the problem-creating provision in the first place"[13]

In response to the report, and in particular to the issue of a 'meaningful relationship' a senior government source said:

"The panel found that shared custody on an equal footing led to lengthy delays in the courts ...They have also rejected the

halfway house of statutory recognition for the need to maintain a meaningful relationship on the basis that the courts would spend ages deciding how to define a meaningful relationship."[14]

This is where pragmatism comes in; the panel believed that parents *should* have a meaningful relationship with their children, indeed they stated that making it a legal right would *"strengthen the principle"* that recognises *"the importance of children having a meaningful relationship with both parents"* but the burden this placed on the court system led to *"doubts about its application"*. Yet as a police officer whimsically pointed out to me recently, legalising theft would also reduce the burden felt by the courts, though this is not a sufficient reason to do it.

So the changes being advocated by fathers' groups may be just, but the effects on the courts would seem to be too drastic for a change to be considered. Pragmatism seems to trump justice in this instance. Is this a good reason not to do what is right and if this is to be used as a justification for maintaining the status quo then surely it is essential to prove that the current state of affairs is the hallmark of efficiency?

Again the FJR was on hand to challenge this assertion when they delivered their final report which stated that *"[presently] cases take far too long"* and *"the family justice system is failing families"*[15] In fact if a picture was to be painted of the family law situation in the U.K. today then the following statistics might be used as the watercolours (all data sourced from the Ministry of Justice, 2013[16]):

The number of children involved in private law applications (in effect applications where there is a dispute over child contact) was 117,500 in 2012 (or 320 children every day). In the fourth quarter of 2012 the average time for a child custody case to go through the courts was 45.1 weeks (although this was acknowledged by the Ministry of Justice to be abnormally low and in fact every other quarter since 2007 has seen cases taking significantly longer than this). So currently, despite a child's welfare being the paramount consideration of the court, parents still have to battle for nigh on a year before their dispute is settled (using the word 'resolved' would have been a stretch too far here) which can only be difficult for the children involved.

This is alarming because it seems as though the justification for not delivering justice is that it would place too great a burden on the court system, yet the courts are delivering extremely poor service presently anyway. Would the situation really be worse for the courts should, say, Baker's presumption of shared parenting be introduced as law? It is difficult to say, given that it has never been trialled in the U.K. Those who argue that it would be worse would claim, as the FJR did, that the courts will be overburdened by having to determine terms such as 'meaningful relationship' or having to allocate the appropriate amount of time with each parent. The facts to support this are, at best, inconclusive.

Around ten years ago Professor Roland Proksch, a doctor of law at the University of Nuremberg, completed a four year research study into the effects of shared parenting in Germany. He concluded that having joint custody as law (as was introduced in Germany a year before the study began) *"reduces oppressive, often highly emotional conflict and expensive court proceedings."*[17] The belief here is that if parents are aware beforehand that they are both to be treated as equals and, therefore, both will be granted equal access to their children (subject to exceptional circumstances such as one being proven to be neglectful, for example) then they will be less likely to litigate as they know it will be costly, drawn out and, ultimately, pointless. The current situation could be argued to be unnecessarily arbitrary, which may lead parents to 'try their luck'. Further to this, those cases that do go to court should be more straightforward as the position to be taken by the court would be absolute, consideration to whether the 'absent' parent should see the children every-other weekend as opposed to every ten days, for example, would never be an issue. In Germany, they chose justice as the basis for law, but by wonderful coincidence, they achieved greater pragmatism as well.

A paternal-grandparent whose time with his grandchild had been significantly affected by the standing of the law in the U.K. recently commented to me that *"if you allow pragmatism to significantly shape law-making then often the end result is that just laws do not ensue. The inherent infighting within these injustices creates unnecessary friction and consequential problems. Perhaps better to bite the bullet, like the Germans, and frame the law with fairness outweighing pragmatism"*.

As it stands, then, it may be seen that the case for change is just but the application of change is being hindered because of a belief that it would lead to delays in the court system. However, the current court system is acknowledged to be lengthy and inefficient and the proposed changes may actually lead to a reduction in case lengths and an increase in efficiency. Hardly a glowing tribute to a justice system lauded as the envy of the world.

A similar ethos – that litigation would actually be reduced if certain changes were adopted – could also be applied to the enforcement of court orders. As was stated in the last chapter, it is not desirable to send a parent to prison due to the effects that it would have on the children. That said, it is also clear that under the current system a resident parent can get away with a lot without any concern for legal reprisals. It may well be the case that a sanction such as changing the residence order from favouring one parent who has been particularly obstructive to favouring the other will be a huge event in the life of the children involved (though not necessarily a negative one). In fact Claire Brissenden, a practicing barrister in family law, wrote an article in 2010 referring to the decision by a judge to change a residence order as a *"judgment of Solomon"* and arguing that they should, therefore, take *"a moment to pause and consider the magnitude of the decision [they] are making when they contemplate a change of residence."*[18]

Brissenden was writing her article on the back of a judgment made in the case of S (A Child) [2010] in which residence was switched. Her stance was clearly one of caution. She went on further to stress that:

"...this is about uprooting a child from possibly the only home they have ever known, from a school, friends and social infrastructure they are familiar with, never mind from a parent to whom they have their primary attachment. The possible consequences of getting it wrong are unthinkable."

The consequences of getting this wrong clearly *are* unthinkable and nobody would advocate causing any child any form of psychological harm. The initial awarding of residence orders to (typically) mothers in the first instance necessarily requires that children be 'uprooted' from what may have involved significantly more time spent with the father before the separation. The breakdown of a relationship often involves the children leaving the *"only home they have ever known"* and this is a strong argument for a presumption of 50/50 shared custody: a requirement would never exist to 'switch' the order as there would be no 'absent' parent in the first place. If Brissenden applied her own logic in the first possible instance, much good might follow.

Given that currently the system does have residence orders and contact orders, they seem of little use if a court is unable to enforce them. It may be viewed as a significant event in a child's life for a residence order to be switched from one parent to the other, but the outcome could be that they end up enjoying time with both parents. Keeping in mind that a judge would only consider switching residence if one of the parents was being obstructive, then this seems a potentially positive outcome. Overall though it should be considered that the enforcement of orders would lead to a reduction in litigation. If resident parents genuinely believed that residence was likely to switch or, worse, that they could face imprisonment for noncompliance of a court order, then the deterrent factor would surely be significant. Parents could not deliberately obstruct without fear of reprisals, so many wouldn't. Because there would be fewer cases of obstruction, both parents would be happier as they would be forced to make the situation work rather than taking the unnecessarily adversarial action of litigation (which would, in turn, be of benefit to the child) and the courts would be less burdened in terms of volume of cases.

Another contested area of family law between reformers and maintainers is the 'secrecy' of the court system (a major argument that rages between fathers' groups and the courts over whether or not the system is biased is made more difficult by the fact that family courts operate in closed sessions). The result is that where courts argue that an outcome is the result of particular circumstances, there are no objective by-standers who can comment. Likewise in the instance an 'absent' parent claims that they were hard-done to, nobody can support or contradict that claim objectively. Consequently some fathers' groups have advocated opening up family courts to the public. For example Fathers 4 Justice has argued that there is a need for *"the removal of an unelected, unaccountable and unsackable judiciary who operate in complete secrecy. Such a system is an affront to a progressive, modern democracy."*[19] Their argument is that the alternative is far more appropriate to a democratic nation as it is easier to scrutinise:

"The introduction of an open, transparent and accountable system of justice predicated on peaceful resolution, not conflict and delay."

Every other court in the land is open for the media and members of the public to monitor and pass their own judgments on. F4J and others would argue that a closed shop with no accountability means that there is little incentive for judges to do justice. Why should family courts be an exception? Well the argument comes down to accountability (as the argument seen so far goes) versus the right to privacy (which is the argument against).

Everybody in the country has a right to a private life guaranteed by the European Convention of Human Rights (ECHR), supported further by the U.K. Human Rights Act 1998 (HRA). Article 8 of ECHR states that:

"1. Everyone has the right to respect for his private and family life, his home and his correspondence.
2. There shall be no interference by a public authority with the exercise of this right except as is in accordance with the law and is necessary in a democratic society in the interests of national security, public safety or the economic well-being of the country, for the prevention of disorder or crime, for the protection of health or morals, or for the protection of rights and freedoms of others. "[20]

The argument follows that family law must be a special case in terms of access by the public because it involves a family's personal details including details of the various members' relationships with one another, correspondence, finances, indiscretions etc. As a solicitor with whom I spoke commented on the issue of opening the family courts to the public:

"There is limited opportunity to do that in cases of financial dispute but in cases involving children they should stay private. It is not in the interest of the children to have their case reported in the media."

'Airing ones dirty laundry in public' has never been something that the British public have been particularly comfortable with. It would be rather unfair then for children to have their personal lives 'aired' because their parents are unable to settle a dispute. That said, there are safeguards against publicising the personal details of children and vulnerable people in every other court setting in the U.K., so why could these not apply to family law? Take the case that inspired Brissenden's article, for example; S (A Child)

[2010]. Most cases that come before courts are titled by surname of the defendant or other interested party. However, in order to safeguard a child in the instance that a case involves them, only their initial is used. The same principle applies to criminal law involving both children and vulnerable adults including any victims of heinous crimes such as rape (only their initials are used to protect their anonymity, for example the recent heavily publicised death of 'Baby P' and subsequent investigations into the parents, carers and shortcomings of social services and Haringey council). The right to privacy can be guaranteed in other court settings so there can be little argument that these safeguards could not be applied to the family courts.

The effects on the courts of transforming family law in the areas of giving parents automatic shared custody on a 50/50 footing, giving children a right to a 'meaningful relationship' with both parents, enforcing orders more robustly than is presently done and opening up the family courts to allow transparency are not, in themselves, reasons to go ahead with changes; there are many other considerations to be made which will be explored in the following chapters. However, one thing that these arguments have demonstrated is that the effects of changes on the courts are certainly no reason *not* to review the law and procedures surrounding the administration of the law. 50/50 shared custody could actually increase the efficiency of the family justice system, stronger enforcement of court orders could reduce the burden of caseload experienced by the courts and opening up proceedings could allow greater transparency and therefore promote the issue of fairness.

Even if, though, all these things were not true, denying people access to justice on the basis of pragmatism is absolutely indefensible. Arguments that the court system would struggle or even collapse if Baker's proposals were introduced does not merit maintaining the current system. In the words of Rawls:

"Justice is the first virtue of social institutions, as truth is of systems of thought. A theory however elegant and economical must be rejected or revised if it is untrue; likewise laws and institutions no matter how efficient and well-arranged must be reformed or abolished if they are unjust...Justice denies that the loss of freedom for some can ever be made right by a greater good shared by others."[21]

Political Suicide

Why successive governments have supported the status quo

"As I leave the second most important job I could ever hold, I cherish even more the first, as a husband and father. Thank you and goodbye."

- Outgoing Prime Minister Gordon Brown, 11th May 2010

Since the passing of TCA successive governments have supported and developed the principles which have led to family law becoming what it is today. There are a couple of possible reasons behind this, the first of which is that governments of all political persuasions (Conservative under Thatcher and Major from the passing of TCA in 1989 until their departure from power in 1997; Labour under Blair and Brown from 1997 until 2010; and presently the Liberal Democrats and Conservatives in coalition together under David Cameron and Nick Clegg) have genuinely supported the law and measures introduced in furtherance of it. This could be due to a belief that, for example, one stable home is better for children than two involved parents, or that the role of mothers is more important than fathers, or it could be due to a belief that the alternatives are unworkable. The other possibility is that politicians do not believe that the status quo is right, but support it anyway. As with any group of people politicians do not (always) make decisions *en bloc* and so these factors have all probably played some role to a greater or lesser extent in the decision making of various individual politicians.

The quote at the start of the chapter – the last lines of the resignation speech of Gordon Brown just after he was defeated in the 2010 general election – suggests, albeit tenuously, that at least some in the higher echelons of authority at Westminster attribute an amount of importance to the role of a father (though critics could always argue that these comments were hollow, made in a moment of hubris as if to suggest that the job from which the Labour leader had just been forcibly removed actually meant less to him than many spectators at the time believed).

Just before that same election the Conservative Party entered into dialogue with F4J and drew up their own blueprint for the reform of family law. On the 8th April 2010 Romsey Conservative Association announced that *"David Cameron and the Conservative Party will make manifesto commitments to reform family law for the first time since the Children Act of 1989, over 20 years ago."*[22]

At the time the Shadow Minister for Justice & Legal Affairs was Henry Bellingham who claimed that *"we have already done a huge amount of research into family law and have reached preliminary conclusions which will form the starting point for major reform."* The term 'major reform' certainly implies an ambitious program. In fact the Conservative Party has conveniently kept a record of the pledge that they made online:

"[Mr. Bellingham] outlined the following principles which the party would follow and they include:

1) A clear definition of contact so couples know what the likely outcome of the case may be, making them less likely to litigate.

2) A legal presumption in favour of automatic shared-contact in the context of joint parental responsibility.
3) An emphasis on early interventions and mediation.
4) Enforceable contact orders including the withdrawal of benefits from parents withholding access.
5) Grandparents to have automatic rights of access to court.
6) A plan to work with the Department of Children, Schools and Families to ensure Cafcass becomes more efficient and is able to devote more time to public law cases and child protection   issues.
7) A pro-active Judiciary with a more efficient handling of cases.
8) A wide consultation with all interested groups with an interim report published by the Autumn of 2010.
9) A commitment to reducing the cost to UK PLC caused by family breakdown and the litigation of family disputes which we believe is intolerable.
10) The most significant consequence of which will be to allow children to reach their true aspirations and potential."

In fact many of these points can be seen to overlap some of those from Baker's blueprint of 2004. This seems to negate the argument that politicians simply accept the fairness of the current state of affairs and that some actually want to see wide-reaching reform. The significance of this statement was that it was not just fringe elements of the Westminster machine that were calling for change, but senior officials in the country's largest political party for which these proposals were to become election manifesto pledges. However, within a few short months of this proposal the two groups responsible for drawing it up – the Conservative Party and F4J – had fallen out over the latter's belief that the former had broken its promises and failed to implement, or even to try to implement, the changes agreed to.

If a manifesto pledge is, in the words of Margaret Thatcher, *"very much the party leader's own statement of policies"*[23] then this commitment should have meant that the leadership of the Conservative Party in the run up to the election in 2010 saw reform of family law as an important policy. In fact we know that there are senior Tories who want to see family law amended to allow fathers a greater role in the upbringing of their children: Former Tory Party leader and current cabinet minister Iain Duncan-Smith is uncharacteristically vocal* in his criticism of what he sees as a culture of *"fatherlessness"* which in turn results in *"poverty and disadvantage"*[24] for the children involved (*uncharacteristic for a politician to be vocal in favour of fathers and uncharacteristic for the self-titled 'Quiet Man' to be vocal at all). In spite of this, though, the agreement that was reached in the April was all but forgotten following the election in the May. F4J claim that the reason for the new government dropping the issue, shortly followed by them supporting the final report of the FJR in 2011, which recommended no changes in the area of child contact, was in order to *"appease women's groups"*.

The full story of how a political party could apparently change its stance within the space of a month requires a consideration of the various governments that have been formed since the passing of TCA in 1989 and, in the context of F4J's comments, their relationships with women's groups. But first to take a look at the conventional wisdom relating to political behaviour which may make politicians susceptible to influence by such pressure groups. This involves some rather crude categorisations but psephologists (those who study elections) enthusiastically use these generalisations as evidence of the likely fortunes of various individuals and parties in the political process, whilst the rest of society often cringes at the logic.

The theory goes that voters are influenced both by short-term and long-term factors. Short term influences may be specific to one election and they include things such as the state of the economy at the time (Roy Jenkins, then Chancellor of the Exchequer, is often blamed for losing Labour the 1970 general election for refusing falsely to inflate the economy using tax cuts – an indication that doing what is right does not work in your favour in politics), the charisma (or otherwise) of the party leaders (The Quiet Man, IDS, was deposed by the Tories prior to an election being called because they felt that the voters would punish them even more than they actually did in the event if he had remained), and the mass media who may or may not be biased one way or another (in the aftermath of the 1992 general election, before which the Conservatives were staring certain defeat in the face yet still managed to come away with a considerable victory, The Sun famously led with a front page headline claiming *It Was The Sun Wot Won It*). Generally, women voters are seen to be short-term voters, less likely to remain loyal to a party than to vote on issues that affect them or the strength or weakness of the party leaders. Female voters are seen, generally, to fall into what psephologists refer to as the 'Rational-Choice Model' of voting, which Andrew Heywood describes as:

"In this view, voting is seen as a rational act, in the sense that individual electors are believed to decide their party preference on the basis of personal self-interest. Rather than

being habitual, a manifestation of broader attachments and allegiances, voting is seen as essentially instrumental: that is, as a means to an end. "[25]

This model is what has given rise to the idea of 'populism' in recent years: leaders, believing that they influence the electorate in a manner disproportionate to the power they will hold when in office (many voters forget that at election time they are voting for a potential MP, rather than a PM) will portray an image of themselves that they believe is 'likeable'. So the public is bombarded with news images of William Hague drinking pints in a pub, Tony Blair's 'Cool Britannia' saga or, more recently, party leaders chomping at the e-bit to tell internet mums what their favourite biscuits are.

Longer-term influences involve things such as class or party loyalty and, it is believed, men are more likely to be influenced by these factors. This fits into what is known as the 'Sociological Model' and again Heywood sums it up nicely:

"The sociological model links voting behaviour to group membership, suggesting that electors tend to adopt a voting pattern that reflects the economic and social position of the group to which they belong...Not uncommonly, party systems have been seen to reflect the class system, with the middle classes providing the electoral base for right-wing parties, and the working classes providing the electoral base for left-wing parties. "

This group of voters explains the existence of the 'safe seat' in elections; all other factors set aside people of a certain region, with similar class-based loyalties may return the same party representative time and again regardless of party performance etc. Most people should be able to find plenty of real life examples where these groupings don't apply and in that sense the model is extremely rough-hewn. That said, the *actual* accuracy of the model is not as important as the *belief* held by many in political positions of power that they do hold the truth about voter behaviour and therefore their actions are directly influenced by them. Consider, then, the logic that would follow if you believed that these presuppositions held true: men contribute to the return to Parliament of a candidate that represents the party that has historically represented their constituency. Women can be affected by events and by the leaders of the parties and, therefore, hold the 'swing vote'. Further, politicians would believe that around 50% of the electorate would vote *en bloc* and therefore winning this vote is crucial to success and future fortunes. A swing vote of half the electorate is something worth fighting for; an habitual vote that is unlikely to change is not.

TCA, then, was passed in 1989 during the last eighteen months of Margaret Thatcher's premiership. She was famously toppled from power by members of her own party who conspired to have Michael Heseltine challenge her for the leadership. For all the determination of that man to succeed Thatcher as Prime Minister, he served only as a stalking horse until she withdrew from the contest, which went on to be won by John Major. Major, consequently, inherited a divided party and the next few years would be an uphill struggle to gain control of it (although there are few that would argue that he ever really did; Tony Blair infamously taunted Major many a time over the dispatch box at Prime Minister's Questions [PMQ] with comments like *"I lead my party, he follows his"* and that Major was *"weak, weak, weak"*).

A series of scandals and rebellions from within his own ranks would haunt Major's leadership and indeed cause him to appear weak (cabinet colleagues being exposed as having extra-marital affairs, the Maastricht Treaty dividing the Conservative Party even more than it already was). So much so that the issue of fathers' rights would never have featured on his radar. The issue was out there – Families Need Fathers was formed in 1974 and had been campaigning for equality ever since – but there are more pertinent reasons than timid leadership that meant that this issue was never going to be an attractive one for Major to tackle. Firstly, in spite of claims made elsewhere in the press, as regards to the 1992 general election it was almost certainly Women Wot Won It. The Conservative Party may have resisted universal suffrage at the end of the 19th and start of the 20th centuries but they have more than benefitted from it ever since. In the words of Geoffrey Wheatcroft *"from the moment they were enfranchised, women voted predominantly Conservative: without them, the Tories would have won far fewer elections in the twentieth century than they did."*[26]

Major needed women, as do all Prime Ministers. That is not to say that he did nothing to offend them. In order to try to assert his authority whilst at the same time demonstrating to the right wing (or Thatcherite, though Major would rue the term) sect of his own party that he was one of them, he launched his 'Back to Basics' campaign in 1993. The idea was to prove to people that he could be tough on crime, that his cabinet did not lack moral integrity (in spite of their publicised indiscretions), and that he could be trusted to handle the economy (in spite of Black Wednesday). Part of Back to Basics was a cut in welfare spending in order to manage recovery from recession. This was seen as an attack on stay-at-home mothers who would lose income in the process. Following the launch of Back to Basics Major came under heavy criticism from women's groups who felt that he was out of touch with the needs of mothers. He needed to keep them onside if he had any chance of surviving through the next election so he was never going to consider another affront by attempting to pass legislation telling mothers that they were not, in fact, more important than fathers. However, as it transpired, women would desert Major in 1997 anyway and help deliver a landslide victory at the election to his new opponent, Tony Blair.

Like his Prime Ministerial predecessor before him, Anthony Charles Lynton Blair won his first general election as the leader of his party on the back of a wave of support from women, although the support in his case was far more overt. This was because it was not just in terms of the popular vote that Blair could claim to have a working mandate supported by females: Following the 1997 general election there were 120 female MPs, more than at any other time in history, and 101 of them represented the Labour Party. There was a heavily publicised photograph of Blair standing outside the Palace of Westminster with 95 of these MPs, leading the press to label them 'The Blair Babes' (a much more benevolent term than the one used to refer their male counterparts, who became known as 'Tony's Cronies'). How could anybody claim that New Labour did not represent the interests of women? They had returned more women than any other party at a single election in history, and five times as many as all the other parties put together in this election.

As Prime Minister Blair was all too aware of the agenda of fathers' groups as the year of his second election victory – 2001 – coincided with the founding of F4J who, through their direct actions campaigns, would go on to target Blair as the most senior political figure of the day. In fact, in an incredible display of audacity, in May 2004 two members of F4J got themselves signed into the House of Commons as guests of a Labour Peer in order to watch PMQ and, during the proceedings, threw purple coloured powder at Blair, subsequently having Parliament suspended and getting themselves arrested.

In spite of being aware of the issue Blair did not act to change the law. It may be that he was vehemently in favour of the status quo. The fact is that it wouldn't have mattered if he wasn't. For all of Tony Blair's determination to shape the way history remembered him (he is the only Prime Minister since Harold Macmillan who was able to pick the date of his departure from office, and this only because he wanted it to be as notable as possible) he was, first and foremost, a pragmatist; arguably far more so than he was a man of principle. This can be seen in his attitude towards Europe: he was, as Prime Minister, a Europhile and passionately in favour of joining the single currency. He wasn't, though, in favour of it enough to put it to the country and risk losing an election on the back of it. He could have forced the issue through; he had a large enough majority in the commons, but with the black cloud of another general election always looming over the horizon, Blair wouldn't risk doing something unpopular, no matter how passionate he was about it. Note also that the statement above says that Tony Blair was a Europhile 'as Prime Minister'. In the 1980's when he first stood for Parliament (unsuccessfully in a by-election in 1982 before standing and winning in the Labour safe seat of Sedgefield in the general election of the following year) he was, according to his local association leaflets, somewhat anti-European (a position which would later be coined 'Eurosceptic') as was the position of the Labour Party during this time. What this goes to show is that however much Blair claimed to be a man of principle, his main principle was that he should be in power. Everything else he claimed to care about could be forgotten if it conflicted with this one, more important, goal. He was for winning and against somebody else winning and he couldn't do it without the support of women. Women had reversed the Tory majority from the 1992 election and women would keep him in power for ten years.

Gordon Brown was another leader not immune to the temptation of courting the 'women's vote'. Shortly after he succeeded Tony Blair as Labour leader and Prime Minister, Brown was advised that his announcement of a focus on core values had caused women to support him and, consequently, he received an 11-point lead over the Tories in the opinion polls during the summer of 2007. Shortly afterwards he was informed that by appointing Harriet Harman – a known feminist – as his deputy leader in the Labour party, seventeen percent of people would be more likely to vote Labour. It hardly needs saying that he took this course of action without a second thought, also going on to shower her with other titles for good measure (chair of the Labour Party, leader of the House of Commons, minister for women). During the campaign for the 2010 election, when Brown had exhausted Labour's boost in the polls caused by the leadership change and he now trailed David Cameron's Conservative Party, he started to make promises to give expectant mothers a legal right to choose where they give birth, in the hope that this would cause women to start queuing up to vote for him.

Brown wasn't the only leader guilty of chasing women during that campaign. Also in the build up to the 2010 general election David Cameron's Conservative Party went to such extreme lengths as having female-only shortlists for their parliamentary candidates in order to demonstrate that he was not sexist to a nation who had been used to ten years of 'Blair's Babes' followed more recently by a female Labour Party Deputy Leader who was, arguably, a stronger leader than her superior. This suggests that Cameron is as susceptible as anybody to feeling the need to court women. Couple this with the Conservative Party being forced into coalition with the Liberal Democrats, who will condemn to the end anybody who stands in the way of their mission to offend as few people as possible, and controversial principles are dead in the water. This coalition of ideologically opposed parties was unlikely, though it seems to support De Tocqueville's observation that *"in politics, shared hatreds are almost always the basis of friendships"*[27], so what is desirable can take a back seat, as long in return something undesirable doesn't occur. In this case a political agenda was sacrificed in the name of keeping the keys to Number 10 away from the Labour Party for five years. Particular issues could still have been fought for (and conceivably won) but history teaches us to pick our battles, and for all the pre-election rhetoric about families being at the 'front and centre' of the Tories' 'Big Society' vision, reforming family law in the way promised to F4J simply was not important enough.

Of course the idea that there is a single 'women's vote' is no more realistic than that there is one 'men's vote' but for whatever reason the modern politician is obsessed with the idea not only that it exists, but that it can be won with a simple pledge to reduce the cost of childcare or some similar proposal. In a political world where winning is everything, something that could lose a party votes is simply unthinkable: as stated, women don't, in reality, vote as one, but male political leaders could not stomach the thought of being accused of being sexist. Those who do speak out on this issue either never make it up the greasy pole or else they are forced to change their stance in time. So the issue may be just, as was discussed in the last chapter, but in politics, 'just' can take a back seat to 'popular'. This is the reason that governments cannot support making family law less discriminatory.

Edmund Burke once warned that *"when leaders choose to make themselves bidders at an auction of popularity, their talents, in the construction of the state, will be of no service. They will become flatterers instead of legislators; the instruments, not the guides, of the state."*[28] In other words, what good is a leader, if all they do is follow?
I think George W. Bush put it nicely when he said *"One of my proudest moments is I didn't sell my soul for the sake of popularity."*[29]
Yes, that was a good moment.

Living with an Equal
Effects of changes on women

"There still aren't nearly enough women in the boardroom... there aren't nearly enough women around the Cabinet table. In every walk of life, whether judiciary, politics or business, there's a lot further to go. My own view is, it isn't enough just to open up and say we will treat everyone equally, when you are starting from such a position of disadvantage."

-   David Cameron, 18th February 2013

When he gave this quote in a speech made during a visit to India, David Cameron wasn't just attempting to align himself closer with the politically-influential women's groups, he was speaking the truth. All evidence shows that women are not paid as much as men and that women hold fewer senior positions than men in every industry, including Cameron's own government. In 2013 only 25% of MPs are female and, worse, there are only five women in a cabinet of 31 people. In the second half of 2012 only 26% of appointments to board level positions in UK businesses went to women[30]. The history of women's plight on the path to equality is a long one and, like any good struggle, is littered with heroes and villains throughout. The feminist movement was born out of a determination by (some) women to have access to the same opportunities as men (incredibly enough, and rather difficult to believe today, not all women embraced the notion that they should have the same rights and chances as men, some going to such lengths as forming their own counter-movements including the *Women's National Anti-Suffrage League*). Feminism involved, but was not limited to, the suffragette movement (in which women, and indeed many men, campaigned for the right of women to vote). It is difficult for most of us living in the 21st Century to consider not giving someone equal status in, say, the workplace on the basis of their gender. However, many women's groups still claim that this is the case and consistent government reports on a 'gender pay gap' and the number of 'women in the boardroom' seem to support the argument that, even in a world that has seen the passing the Equal Pay Act 1970, Sex Discrimination Act 1975 and the Equality Act 2010, men still seem to go further and earn more than women in the workplace.

One of the earliest western writers on equality was John Stuart Mill whose works in the mid-19th Century would inspire generations of women to stand up and be counted. Women desperate for equality took desperate measures. Emily Davison is famous for being a militant suffragette who eventually died for the cause having been hit by the King's Horse during the Epsom Derby in 1913 (whether it was 'suicide for the cause' or a publicity stunt-gone-wrong is unclear, though hardly the point; Davison did die and her legacy was to announce to the men in power-circles that her cause was serious and needed to be addressed). For years since she has been hailed by some as a feminist hero, bravely using her voice in a world controlled by men. Other factions have since labelled her a 'loon' or simply a criminal, citing that by 1912 she had been imprisoned several times for such acts as obstruction, stone throwing, smashing windows, arson and, most notably, assaulting a vicar whom she mistook to be David Lloyd-George. However, even those who argue against Davison's actions may well support the motive, just not the means.

How incredible, then, that one hundred years later similar acts are taking place to those Davison committed in order to achieve similar ends. One hundred years after Davison's ultimate sacrifice, in June 2013, a man was charged with criminal damage after spray-painting the word 'help' over a Jubilee portrait of the Queen hung at Westminster Abbey[31]. The man was campaigning for the right to see his children having separated from their mother. Criminal damage, unlawful means to achieve an end in the form of equality, we have seen this before. J.S. Mill wrote an essay in 1869 entitled 'The subjection of women' in which one of his more powerful passages was as follows:

"...the generality of the male sex cannot yet tolerate the idea of living with an equal. Were it not for that, I think that almost every one, in the existing state of opinion in politics and political economy, would admit the injustice of excluding half the human race from the greater number of lucrative occupations...ordaining from their birth either that they are not, and cannot by any possibility become, fit for employments which are legally open to the stupidest and basest of the other sex"[32]

Mill was right, of course, and 150 years later the thought of denying opportunities to women on the basis of their gender is abhorrent to most of us, and unlawful in any case. This is largely thanks to the work of the feminist movement. Now reconsider Mill's quote but switch the words 'employments' and 'occupations' with the word 'childcare'. Should men, on the basis of their gender (or *"ordaining from their birth"*) be excluded from that which the most unfit women are legally included? This is to stray from the point somewhat: The consideration in this book so far has been focused around the inequalities of family law and how this affects fathers but for this chapter the consideration will be how the current situation affects women and how the lives of women, and particularly mothers, would be influenced if family law was reformed to treat parents equally. But the point above at least demonstrates that the 'feminist' ideals are still highly relevant today, even if they are for arguing the other side of the case.

The subordination of women has been attributed by some academics to the make-up of capitalist society and the laws that govern it (most of which were written by men), which, it is argued, will never allow women equal status. The belief lies in a perceived conflict between feminine care- and masculine justice-based views on morality. The law (generally) reflects a masculine-type standpoint which states that there are set rules and that breaches of those rules should be objectively dealt with. The idea is that this will equate to greater fairness (if two people committing the same crime are punished in the same way then there is no room for subjective prejudices). However, when dealing with any given situation women tend to apply what has come to be known as care-based morality; that is they will try to empathise with the subject and may prefer to exert discretion. The feminist argument is that because the legal, political and business systems are so weighted towards masculine-justice, rather than feminine-care, women are naturally at a disadvantage. Joan Tronto, a twentieth century theorist, stated that political ideas of power and justice make society believe that women are 'naturally' mothers, the result being that they are *"seen as fit only for functional roles, are seen as utterly different from the privileged selves who have dismissed them, and are not thought of as potential equals* "[33]. These deep rooted political ideas will inevitably prevent women from gaining power because, Tronto believes, due to centuries of masculine domination the West is systemically masculine and even if feminine-care viewpoints were given a voice they would always be considered from this masculine-justice-based context.

Tronto's argument is hard to deny; although she uses the argument to demonstrate women's difficulty in achieving the same status in society as men, many men in the West feel that the assumption of women as primary carers works against *them*. Coming back to family law I recently spoke with a solicitor who stated that in custody cases, the reason that children so often end up living with their mothers is a simple one:

"The thinking is that children are best with their mother on a psychological and emotional basis whereas in North America they tend to see psychological and emotional benefits as coming from the child seeing both parents."

He explained that this was because mothers are seen here in the U.K. as more nurturing, and better carers than fathers. Equal rights should have to work both ways but this field at least illustrates that Tronto's point may be accurate: women are stigmatised as carers to such an extent that men get little consideration when it comes to custody of their children.

The family law situation in the UK is indicative of the inherent view of all involved in law-making that women are primarily carers. Due to the suffragette movement women have equal access to politics, women have equal access to education, pay laws are bringing women's salaries closer in line to men's. Yet the one aspect of law which consistently favours the *woman* simultaneously appears to hinder the advancement of *women*. This, it seems, is the last obstacle to equality, but in more ways than the obvious one. That is to say that family law creates conspicuous inequalities between men and women, but there are also some less discernible inequalities which are caused by the current situation. These inequalities are those which affect women and give today's 'second-wave feminists' so much to feel aggrieved about.

The logic is as follows: TCA states that the best interests of the child is paramount; current thinking is that children are better off with one stable home than two involved parents; women are stigmatised as 'carers' and therefore the child is placed in the care of mothers, rather than fathers. The fact that women are branded as carers, however, can be shown to *cause* the 'gender pay gap' and the lack of women in senior positions within industry that second-wave feminists denounce the injustices of so vehemently.

At the end of 2012 the Trade Union Congress (TUC) published a study highlighting that there is a *"36% pay gap"* between people in part time work and people in full time work, whereby 'part-timers' will earn over a third less per hour than their full time colleagues (this latter qualification is important because it emphasised that part-time workers were earning less for the same number of hours worked, not just earning less for working fewer hours, which nobody in their right minds would have a problem with). This was not the end of the matter, though, because it seemed that women were disproportionately affected by this anomaly. In fact the study showed that *"there are more than eight million part-time workers in the UK, nearly three-quarters of whom are female and a large number live in poverty.* "[34]

If three quarters of part time workers are female, this suggests from the numbers above (and a U.K. workforce of around 30 million people[35]) that around 40% of women in the workplace are employed on a part-time basis. This is a huge number. The reasons why are explained further by Frances O'Grady, General Secretary Designate of the TUC in commenting on their own report: *"Most women become part-time workers to balance work and caring responsibilities."*

It seems, then, that the TUC, and many others, believe that women are unfairly hindered at work because of their role as carers to children outside of work. The solution, according to the TUC, is greater job sharing opportunities at higher level positions and a commitment by firms to honour the living wage. These are credible ideas which should be taken forward because part-time work is becoming more common and individuals should not be forced to earn less (particularly not below the poverty line) due to their family commitments.

That said, there is the other change, already discussed in previous chapters, which could be introduced as a further measure to help reduce the gender pay-gap, which should consequently resolve more than one injustice. Purely in consideration of the effects that reforming family law to give both parents equal footing would have on women, the consequences would be threefold.

Firstly, and arguably the main effect, is that if two separating parents split the time with their children equally, then the would-be-resident parent will have more time available to work. If a parent is a 'single parent' then often they are forced to work part-time in order to accommodate childcare. This results in them receiving lower total incomes but also falling into the trap of receiving a lower hourly rate as already outlined. For many 'single parents' the alternative is to work full-time and pay for childcare, but this is extremely costly and usually works out to be unaffordable. If childcare was 'free', however, in the form of the would-be-absent parent then this would alleviate some of the financial burden felt by the would-be-resident parent. In other words, by refusing to allow one parent equal access to their children, the courts and the family law system are causing financial hardships for the other parent.

In recent years the U.K. economy has been in-and-out of recession and the government's response has been to reduce its own outgoings including in welfare spending. In fact, in 2013 the government is introducing the Universal Credit, which is to replace existing benefits, simplify the system, make it fairer but also, in the words of Work and Pensions Secretary Iain Duncan Smith, *"make work pay"*. The idea is that a person out of work should not be entitled to a larger income from the state than one in work, in otherwise similar circumstances. In March 2012 during the announcement of the conception of the Universal Credit, The Department of Work and Pensions (DWP) asserted that *"...lone parents will be better off under a system which will incentivise work and make work pay"*[36]. This means that in future lower income parents will have to work longer hours in order to receive a similar income to what they are used to now, so free childcare would go a long way to assisting with the pressures that this will cause. With regard to middle- and higher- income families, allowing more time for work will increase the salary of the parent concerned (for obvious reasons) but it will also prevent them, or rather reduce the risk of them, falling into the trap of receiving a lower hourly rate than their colleagues simply because they work fewer hours. The financial benefits for the would-be-resident parent could be enormous if the law was reformed. It seems to reiterate the point already made that family law favours mothers, whilst simultaneously disempowering them.

Although this benefit would be significant in itself, as stated sometime earlier, it is only one of three consequences that would likely ensue if the law was to be changed.

The second benefit that women would see stems from the likelihood that more men would end up working part-time as opposed to full-time. The logic is that rather than women being forced into part-time work because of childcare commitments, mothers and fathers could share the responsibility (it would seem inappropriate to use the word 'burden' here, when we are assuming that both parents *want* access to their children) and this would mean that on the one hand women could be free to work longer hours but on the other hand men may be required to work fewer hours (it is not unreasonable to suggest that both parents could work full time and manage their childcare commitments, which will be explored more in the next chapter, but it is likely that for many families it may work out more practical for both parents to reduce their hours slightly). Although this means that fathers may well lose some income, it seems fairer that both parents should reduce their hours by a small amount, rather than one having to cut theirs, and therefore their income, significantly to care for a family that they may struggle to support financially.

Men having to reduce their hours would produce two side-effects. The first is that these men would be taking, effectively, a pay cut, bringing them closer in line with the pay of part-time workers, most of whom are women. If the

TUC study mentioned earlier is correct, 75% of part-time workers are women. If this was brought down closer to 50%, then the 'gender pay gap' will have been significantly reduced, if not removed. The second side-effect would be that if both parents work slightly fewer hours, rather than one full-time and one part-time, that would mean, in effect, that there would be more part-time workers than there are currently. This means that the hourly pay rate awarded to part-time workers, so far below that of their full-time colleagues because they are viewed almost as a second-class workforce, would be put under extreme pressure for review. According to the Office for National Statistics, full-time workers in the U.K. earn an average of £12.76 per hour, whereas part-time workers earn an average of £8.01[37]. If the number of part-time workers rose then employers would be forced to consider treating them more favourably than they currently do, beginning with paying them similar amounts for similar work.

This leads nicely onto the third effect for women of changing family law, which is that it would likely increase the number of 'women in the boardroom' for the very same reason; that even those working part-time would likely be viewed with more respect than they currently seem to be. If a workforce is made up largely, or even mostly, of part-time workers then senior management would have little choice but to promote from within this faction. And if women make up a significant bulk of part-timers then surely this will be to their benefit. It could, conceivably be argued that prejudicial senior management would still find a way to discriminate against part-time workers that they regard as second-class, but again, reforming family law would still benefit women in this respect. That is to say that if a consequence of reformation, as has been argued, would be that more men would be channelled into part-time hours, then that means that *fewer* men would be available for promotion to the higher echelons of management, if only full-time workers are considered, which proportionally increases the chances of promotion for women. The TUC's point that more businesses should consider job sharing options for senior positions in order to encourage part-time workers to strive for promotion has a good deal of merit, increasing the part-time workforce is one way to convince employers that this action is necessary.

Whether it is to avoid hypocrisy (because the values of equality which are at the heart of feminism apply as much to men as they do to women), to promote the economic interests of women (so that they are more independent, less reliant on support from the state or from a man, have more time to work and generate an income of their own) or to reduce the apparent inequality between the sexes in the workplace, women's groups should all advocate reforming family law to treat parents equally. If feminism is to achieve all that was hoped in the days of Emily Davison or J.S. Mill, and all that is hoped by today's second-wave feminists, then equality surely starts with reforming the area of law that overtly labels women as 'carers' rather than 'equals'; the one area of law where discrimination is not only accepted, but actively promoted and apparently cherished by those who administer justice.

De-industrial Revolution

Effects of changes on business, benefits and the public purse

"The UK was the first nation to industrialise and was also the first nation to undergo a process of de-industrialisation... The employment relationship has become less homogenous. The full-time, 9-to-5 job with open-ended employee status is less common than it was in the past"

- Chartered Institute of Personnel & Development, July 2013[38]

The effects of delivering Baker's proposals as a blueprint for family law on business, benefits and the public purse could be wide-ranging. To consider business in isolation it is necessary to consider how organisations are affected by the status quo, and how this would change if the law was reformed. This was touched on in the last chapter in terms of men and women in the workplace but will be explored further here. In dealing with benefits, the welfare system is alleged to cost U.K. PLC over £200bn per annum[39] so we need to look at how much of that is affected by family law and excogitate whether this would change for better or worse if the law was reformed. As for the public purse this is largely affected by benefits but also the cost of administering family law today, which again would surely be changed one way or the other as the law alters.

As was discussed in the last chapter, far more women work part-time than men do, and if genuine equality is to be achieved in family law then this would need to change to accommodate it (arguably cause and effect are being confused here, depending on the agenda of those considering them. Proponents of reforming family law would, as per the last chapter, acknowledge that more men would need to work part-time to facilitate the changing roles, whereas second-wave feminists and supporters of the dismantling of the 'glass ceiling' should be arguing that family law needs to change in order to accommodate *this*. One thing that is certain is that the two are mutually dependent and fundamental changes to one will transform society as we know it). Changes to employment demographics could take the form of more women working full-time, more men working part-time, or some of both. However, it is not always feasible for parents to work part- as opposed to full-time, particularly in a world with ever-increasing costs where making ends meet is arguably more difficult than it once was. It may often be the case that, should family law be reformed to give parents an equal share of time with their children, both parents will still need to work upwards of forty hours per week to cover their respective costs of living. If both parents work at similar times of day to each other then childcare may become difficult, or even impossible to arrange whilst simultaneously balancing their time with their children.

If we are considering that men and women are to be treated equally in the workplace in this hypothetical future then this scenario will be relatively common. The only options left available to parents in such a situation would be flexible working, which can be one (or more) of seven possible working practices. Two of these are working part-time and job sharing, which usually go hand in hand and the benefits/drawbacks of which were discussed in the last chapter. The other five are working from home (speaks for itself), compressed hours (working the same number of hours but over fewer days), flexitime (the employee chooses when to start and end work but must work certain 'core hours' as defined by the organisation), annualised hours (the employee must work a certain number of hours over a year but they decide when they do them) and staggered hours (the employee has different start, finish and break times from other colleagues).

Working practices such as these would be essential to any family after a breakdown (and could also have major benefits to a traditional nuclear family) if both parents are to take a full and active role in the upbringing of their children. For this to be possible, though, employment legislation may need amending. The reality is that it would probably become more commonplace if family law was to be reformed simply because this would cause a cultural transformation to such an extent that a huge proportion of the workforce would, almost overnight, require flexible working and so employers (or any employers wishing to retain staff and lower their organisation's attrition rates) would have to respond by accommodating the needs of their employees. The current law regarding flexible working states only that *"anyone can ask their employer to work flexibly"* but that *"your employer doesn't have to agree to the request."*[40]

This makes sense in practice as there will always be industries in which flexible working cannot be facilitated whilst keeping a business profitable, and some requests for flexible working may well be unreasonable, so an employer should retain an amount of discretion. That notwithstanding there is always scope for laws to encourage flexible working, or indeed any initiatives that can help families. Many organisations nowadays are more open to accommodating alternative working practices simply because they can see the benefit that it presents to their organisations; in a globalising world, many businesses have to stay open for longer hours and over a greater number of days just to compete, so individuals who offer to work outside of the regimented 9-5 routine can often be an asset.

Actually, due to completely unrelated factors, the U.K. is already changing economically in a way that would better accommodate single parents and broken families. The quote from the CIPD at the start of the chapter is accurate; over the past century the U.K. has undergone a de-industrial revolution which has seen the make-up of the workforce and the composition of employment alter drastically from a mainly industry-based, to a mainly service based economy. In 1911 nearly 40% of the U.K. workforce was employed in manufacturing, in 2011 the figure was lower than 10%. Conversely in 2011 over 80% of workers were employed in the services sector.[41]

This is due to increased wealth allowing people to spend more on ('luxury') services rather than just the necessities. It also coincides with a lower profitability in manufacturing. The consequences of this shift in industries is that these new services (restaurants, shops, gyms, leisure centres, spas, hotels, bars, nightclubs etc.) actually *require* flexible working in order that they be accessible by everyone (including those other people working in other flexible-working industries!). Even established sectors do not always respect the traditional 9-5, Monday to Friday, working arrangements. For example, in banking and finance nearly every major institution has their main contact operations (call centres) open on evenings, weekends and, you guessed it, bank holidays (thereby challenging the term somewhat), albeit their high street operations do not tend to conform to this trend. The other factor that has assisted in this change from an industry- to a service-based economy is, as was highlighted in the last chapter, the rise of women in the workforce. Since the Second World War women have taken up a much larger role in the workplace (during the twentieth century women went from making up 29% to 46% of the U.K. workforce[42]) but there was no similar-scaled counterbalancing of men in the home.

So flexible working has become more prominent largely as a result of the changes to the constitution of U.K. businesses and the employment market, but its implications can be very positive not just for the individuals who take it up, but for their employers and the economy as a whole. In July 2013 the Royal Society for the encouragement of Arts, Manufactures and Commerce (RSA) published a report that researched flexible working and which they were commissioned to produce by Vodafone. The report, known as The Flex Factor Report, claimed the following[43]:

- *The majority (77 percent) of UK employees work in organisations that provide some kind of flexible working. [p.5]*
- *Organisational benefits [to flexible working]*
  - *Innovation: a correlation between innovative capacity and flexibility*
  - *Productivity: 5.1 productive hours per week gained per employee, equating to c. £4200 per annum per employee*
  - *Cost savings; £650 per annum/per employee saving on desk space; £100 on printing... [p.5-p.6]*
- *Indicative potential national benefits*
  - *Value of productive hours gained: £6.9bn*

     o   *Workstation savings: £1.1bn*
     o   *Printing cost savings: £150m [p.6]*

The benefit to the family of flexible working arrangements is its single most important quality. As The Flex Factor Report further stated:

"Flexible working appears to allow people to fulfil their parenting and caring roles, as well as pursue wider interests and participate in the life of their local community.
The main gain for employees is the greater opportunities to fit other commitments and activities in with work and make better use of their free time. It is particularly helpful for people caring for children or other dependants..."

So flexible working taken up by employees on a much larger scale than it is at the moment would be a further consequence of reforming family law. As has been shown though, this is not just possible but actually desirable from a productivity and economic point of view. Traditional working – 9-5 – is all but dead as employers realise that their strengths lie in their ability to keep trading over more hours. The reform of family law would simply promote a larger uptake of a trend that is occurring anyway.

There are, however, further economic benefits to reforming family law than that business would run more efficiently. If the effects discussed in the last chapter – that reforming family law to give parents equal rights and responsibilities in the upbringing of their children – were to come to fruition, and would-be-resident parents are lifted out of a poverty that they may currently be trapped in and then the consequences for the Treasury could be huge savings on welfare payments. This was the second consideration stated earlier. It may be the case, as stated in the last chapter, that six million women in the U.K. workforce work part-time, largely due to childcare needs, but this is only the tip of the iceberg when it comes to the effects on the taxpayer. Currently single parents are entitled to a plethora of different welfare benefits from the U.K. Treasury in order to assist with the financial burden of raising a child on one income. These are as follows:

Income Support

This is available to those who work fewer that sixteen hours per week. Typically this is taken up by lone parents who need to care for their children and, even when the children get to school age, the parent cannot work outside of school hours. This often means that if a child is to be dropped at school at 9 a.m. and collected at 3 p.m. then a parent has the option of working between 10 a.m. and 2 p.m. to allow time for travel. This gives them a maximum of 20 hours per week to work, and often it is less than this, not least because working those extra four hours would lead to an individual losing £58 per week income support. If the average part-time wage is £8.01 as per the last chapter, then working the extra hours makes little financial sense to parents. The cost of income support to the U.K. taxpayer in 2012 was £6.92bn[44]. Clearly if more would-be-absent parents could be encouraged to spend more time with their children, then more would-be-resident parents could spend more time in work and reduce the burden to the taxpayer.

Jobseekers Allowance (JSA)

This is available to those who want to work and are actively looking for work. For lone parents this can mean years of searching for a job that can fit into the criteria stated above of school-hours only, never able to find one because their needs are too specific. Again, this could be alleviated by giving non-resident parents a more active role. The restrictiveness of looking for work within that narrow time frame could be alleviated if the would-be-absent parent was able to see their children for eighty four hours (half) per week. According to the Office for National Statistics *"there were 150,280 JSA lone parent claimants at May 2013"* which, at £71.70 per week (the allowance awarded to a single parent aged over 18, which is more than that which is awarded to an unemployed non-parent, according to www.gov.uk) amounts to £10,775,076 per annum.

Child Tax Credit (CTC)

CTC is available to those charged with caring for a child, whether working or not, provided their income is not above a certain limit (there are different limits for different circumstances but for a family with one child who does not suffer from a disability and who do not pay for any childcare, the limit is £26,000). CTC can be awarded at up to £2,720 per child, per annum. Again, increasing the incomes of the various parents/guardians/carers of these children will allow the treasury to reduce its bill in this area; even if parents do not increase their incomes enough not to be entitled to CTC, the amount payable is income-dependent so it can be reduced if incomes increase.

Working Tax Credit (WTC)

WTC is available to assist those who work but receive lower incomes. The idea is that without it, people would be less inclined to work because that would result in their CTC being reduced. Therefore in order to encourage people into gainful employment, the state provides assistance, the standard amount of which is £1,970 per annum, but can be lower depending on the income of the claimant. Again this means that allowing parents to earn more should reduce the burden placed on the state.

As of October 2013 all of these benefits will be replaced by the Universal Credit, which is designed to be less confusing (who wants to learn all the above terms when they could just learn one?), have less stigma attached (people may know that an individual claims benefits from the welfare state but they needn't know why or what for) and run more cost effectively (the same criteria are used, but rather than inputting details onto four different systems to work out the four benefit amounts, it is all computed as one and a final sum calculated and paid out). However, because the calculations will be roughly the same the results should be similar. According to the DWP benefit and tax credit spending in Great Britain was at £197 billion in 2012/13. Further, between the years 1997/98 and 2012/13 *"Expenditure on tax credits and their equivalent benefits increased by 343 per cent in real terms"*.[45]

An expenditure bill of £0 on welfare payments will never be achievable, but it should be something to be aspired towards and if there are options that can help the country get closer to this target, then they should surely be worthy of consideration.

The third aspect to be discussed was the cost of administering family law today, in comparison with what it would cost under a reformed system. According to F4J *"in 2011, the Family Justice System cost the taxpayer £800 million"*[46]. This figure includes the costs of judges' salaries, clerks' salaries, administration, overheads, legal aid etc. The court system has already been shown to be unnecessarily inefficient and this astronomical cost is simply a by-product of that culture. The argument put forth in chapter 2 stated that there were two reforms in particular which could be made in family law that would directly impact upon the debility of the court system. Firstly, a presumption of 50/50 shared custody would reduce litigation as would-be-absent parents who may otherwise feel they have nothing to lose by going to court would not need to, and would-be-resident parents wouldn't feel as confident that the court will simply bend to their will, so both parties could avoid litigation safe in the knowledge that they know what they outcome would be in advance. As the study by Dr. Proksch concluded when considering the before-and-after effects of the reform to law enacted in Germany, a presumption of shared custody did curtail litigation. So this would reduce the nigh-on year-long average of court custody cases and, consequently, the cost of administering those cases.

Secondly, a commitment by the court to enforce its own orders on the first time of being breached would eliminate the need for parents to take their opposite numbers to court over breaches $2,3,4...\infty$ times, again eliminating a waste of time, resources and, ultimately, money.

Based on the above we can assume that reforming family law would have three economic consequences:

1. **Flexible working**. The sheer volume of workers that would have childcare considerations would be such that flexible working would become a standard practice in most organisations. The claims made in The Flex Factor Report suggest that the economy could benefit from

flexible working alone to the sum of £9.15bn per annum (which would only be increased by more people being able to access employment due to the childcare burden being shared between parents, rather than carried by one).

2. **Welfare bill**. This is likely to reduce due to more would-be-resident parents being able to enter employment or extend their hours if they are already employed, which should lead to some very significant savings to the U.K. taxpayer. In 2012 there were 17.9 million families in the U.K. claiming benefits relating to children[47]. Not all of these welfare payments could be removed as there will always be people earning little over minimum wage on reduced hours, not least because throughout this book we have been working on the presumption that both parents *want* to be involved with their children which, alas, is not always the case (though the number of fathers 'held back' from seeing their children is much larger than the numbers who are uninterested, but that is a discussion for another book). That said, there is an enormous amount being paid out which could be cut and quite significantly.

3. **Court Costs**. £800 million spent every year hearing cases because parents have no way of knowing what the precedents are for their circumstances due to the secrecy of the courts, parents have to litigate against each other over and over because the courts are presently unwilling to enforce their own rulings, and parents feeling the need to fight each other because neither have anything to lose by doing so, yet neither gains anything either. This figure should not be as high as it is and this is by far the most avoidable expense to the taxpayer of all those considered. Whereas the other require behavioural changes to the parties involved (the receptiveness of organisations to

flexible working, or the openness of people to taking on more work), this bill would be reduced immediately upon the passing of legislation amending TCA to acknowledge both parents as equals.

The financial benefits, then, cannot be ignored. The knock-on effects are likely to be even greater in the longer term as children are brought up in more prosperous households and, more importantly, households in which their main role models are not encouraged to fight each other in court. The life chances for these children will surely be greater, but this will be explored more later on. For now the temporary conclusion can be that if it is possible to show that parents would benefit financially, the economy would benefit as a whole and organisations could be made stronger as a (very) indirect by-product, then on top of the arguments discussed already about justice and fairness, the reasons for maintaining the status quo are looking very patchy indeed. However, judgment should not be passed prematurely, for the most important consequence of change is still to be considered.

'Tax on Fatherhood'
Effects of changes on child support

"Too many parents have come to see the CSA as the default option for arranging maintenance. It is our view that the better way to secure an effective maintenance arrangement, including (but not limited to) financial maintenance, is to support parents to reach their own arrangements wherever possible..."

- Department for Work and Pensions, 2012[48]

The Child Support Agency (CSA) was launched on 5th April 1993 in order to enforce the laws laid out in The Child Support Act (TCSA) of 1991. It is the public-facing or delivery arm of the Department for Work and Pensions' Child Maintenance Group (which was, until 2012 known as the Child Maintenance and Enforcement Commission). The CSA's dual functions were to calculate the amount of child support that the absent parent should pay to the resident parent and to collect and enforce those payments. They can become involved in any case at the request of one (or both) parent(s). It has had a troubled history since its inception; in its first year it received over 1,000 complaints[49], on Fathers' Day 1994 fathers' groups took to the streets to campaign against the CSA making *"valid arguments for the rights of fathers who have been victimised by the law and their previous partners, and now by the CSA"*[50] according to the *Independent*. In October of that year it became disclosed that 40% of payments ordered by the CSA had been miscalculated, a fact which angered the affected parties even more the following year, when the figure rose to over 50%.

In 1996 the CSA found that contrary to achieving one of its two primary functions of enforcing and collecting payments, it had over £1bn in unpaid maintenance on its books. In 1997 they opened their call centres from 7 a.m. until 9 p.m., six days per week in an attempt to clear this backlog (and thereby becoming an employer that promoted flexible working, which is arguably one of its strongest contributions to parenting to date). By 2002 there was still £1bn worth of arrears to the CSA.

In April 2003 the Agency launched a new telephone and computer network at a cost of £456 million which was intended to make its functions run more smoothly and therefore provide a better service to parents. However, five months later in the November the DWP admitted that only 4% of the 150,000 new people who had applied for maintenance since the launch had received any money at all.

In July 2004 a committee of MPs announced their findings that 75,000 maintenance cases had been 'lost' in the new computer system, there was a backlog of 170,000 cases yet to be processed and this figure was growing by around 10,000 cases every month.

Today the total arrears figure is at around £3.8bn.

The way that child maintenance is calculated through the CSA is fairly straightforward. For a separated couple who have one child the absent parent is required to pay the resident parent 15% of his or her net income. Where the parents have two children the absent parent must pay the resident parent 20% of their net income and where they have three or more children the figure is 25%. These amounts can be reduced if the child spends more than one night per week with the absent parent. For example, an absent parent who is allowed to see his or her child under once a week is required to pay 15% of their salary to a resident parent, whereas if that stay is increased to 1-2 nights per week then the figure drops to 12.5%. As stated in chapter one, though, it is the terms 'resident parent' and 'absent parent' which matter when it comes to determining who pays whom (and someone always *has* to pay). If residence is awarded, say, to the mother, but a father has the child live with him more than half the time and pays for all food and clothing etc., he will still be required to pay the mother 5.75% of his income. The upshot of all this is that the system is often not just about one parent trying to hurt the other emotionally; when resident parents fight to restrict the access of non-resident parents they are actually fighting for more money.

Consider the following case study:

Jim and Jen have been together for five years and have a two year old child together named Joanne. Jim is an office administrator earning £18,000 per annum. Jen is an accountant at the same firm making £35,000 per annum. Jim discovers that Jen has been having an extra-marital affair but offers to work through it, however Jen is uninterested. She takes Joanne and leaves the family home to live with her new partner. A short time later because the two are in dispute over finances, Jen becomes difficult over Jim's access to Joanne, often telling him he can see her then making her unavailable, other times simply refusing to allow him to see her. Jim then takes Jen to court over residence of Joanne.

Before the case Jim's solicitor tells him that he needs to find an agreement he can live with and take it, because a court will not grant residence to a father over a mother. But Jim is paying the solicitor's fees so he gladly argues Jim's case, in spite of being convinced that the position is unachievable. Jim tells the court that the house in which he is living is the only home that Joanne has ever known, that displacing her could be psychologically damaging, that Jen has been acting unreasonably in restricting access and that Jen cannot possibly have Joanne's best interests at heart because she had an affair and refused to work through their issues. When the case looks like it may not be going Jim's way he further argues that Jen's job requires her to work long hours and therefore she cannot provide the attention to caring for Joanne that he could offer. The court goes on to grant residence to Jen, giving Jim a contact order that he is able to see Joanne for two nights every other weekend and one evening a week. A child is best off psychologically and emotionally with its mother.

Six months later Jim is in court again, this time over child maintenance. The CSA have been demanding payments from him at a rate of 15% of his salary, which he couldn't afford with a house to pay for on one income. He was certain that by taking the matter to a judge, the reasonableness of his position would be obvious: his ex-wife earns nearly double what he does, surely she should contribute more? The judge told Jim during the case that the income of the resident parent is irrelevant to matters concerning child maintenance. Further, if Jim is only having his daughter stay at his house for the equivalent of one night in seven, then he must be required to pay for half the costs during the other six nights. Jim argued that he wanted to see his daughter more, that she could live with him, but he wasn't allowed. That, the judge replied, was irrelevant to that hearing as it was decided months earlier.

In the above scenario Jim did nothing wrong, he was forcibly separated from his child by his ex-partner, then told by a court that his access was to be restricted to such an extent that he would become someone Joanne knows on a casual basis, rather than a fully involved parent. Furthermore he was then ordered that he would have to pay more money to Jen for the privilege of not seeing his daughter, because that is how child maintenance works. Jen's finances are not considered at all, and the more the absent parent is restricted, the more they have to pay out in cash. This scenario is far from unusual and aside from the obvious injustice of a parent's access to their children being restricted, the CSA actually facilitates the bias they face. The fact that parents who are told by the courts that they may not have as much time with their children as they would like or did have prior to their family breakdown are then forced to pay *more* to the resident parent is what has led F4J to label CSA as a *"tax"*. Their full opinion on the CSA is documented on their website:

"Child Support is a tax on fatherhood. Fathers who fail to pay the CSA have driving licenses and passports removed, some are sent to jail and many tragically commit suicide. By paying child support you are supporting a broken, inefficient and unjust system that discriminates against you on the basis of your gender. It does not support children as the money goes straight to the government, not dependants [sic]. *Child support sustains and encourages a system that denies children access to their fathers. The reality is that without equal rights and responsibilities for fathers, the child support system is doomed to failure ... As the law stands, a father can abandon his children tomorrow, provided he pays."*[51]

This scathing attack almost seems hyperbolic at first glance, until it is considered in the context of scenarios such as that of Jim and Jen, above. This is people's families and their lives that are being dispensed with by the state with bewildering indifference. The displeasure of most fathers' groups with the CSA comes from one of those all-too-common unintended consequences of a seemingly well-intended concept. The idea of having a Child Support Agency to manage and enforce the payments of support from one parent to another came from the conviction of lawmakers that irresponsible parents (terms such as 'Deadbeat Dad' often get used in this context) should be held to account and not allowed to leave their children's more responsible parent struggling to make ends meet. There is little dispute that this is a noble cause. However, by legislating that the less time a parent spends with their child the more they should pay (as was the case with TCSA, 1991) just two years after legislating that *the child's welfare shall be the court's paramount consideration* (as per TCA, 1989) in the context of a belief that children's welfare is best served by having one home, what the government has actually done is create a financial incentive for resident parents to restrict the contact of non-resident parents with their children, and fight through court to keep it that way!

The child maintenance system is failing both families and the public at large in other ways aside from making family breakdown more adversarial, and these further issues would also be resolved by changing family law in favour of equality.

Considering the efficiency of the Child Maintenance Group, this could almost certainly be improved by reforming the law in the ways discussed in previous chapters. When reviewing the cost of running the Child Maintenance and Enforcement Commission (CMEC; the whole operation relating to child support within the DWP, replaced in 2012 with the Child Maintenance Group) the House of Commons Committee of Public Accounts concluded that:

"The Commission's spending has fallen from £610 million in 2008-09 to £517 million in 2010-11. However, the Commission spends 56 pence for every £1 of maintenance collected, compared to the comparable organisation in Australia, which spends the equivalent of just 35 pence for every £1 it collects. Around half of this gap of 21 pence per pound can be explained by the different policy approach adopted in each country."[52]

The different policy approach adopted in each country could account for a saving of around half of the 21 pence in the pound difference for CMEC, which at £517 million per annum, means a saving of over £54 million every year. So what is this *"different policy approach"*?

In 2006 the Australian Parliament passed the Family Law Amendment (Shared Parental Responsibility) Act, which substantially altered family law in that country. It had the effects of increasing the focus on the rights of children to have a meaningful relationship with both parents; encouraging parents to share responsibility for their children equally after separation; and a presumption of equal shared responsibility and access to the child by the parents following separation, unless they agree otherwise. The effect that this has had on Australian family law is remarkable, and will be explored in more detail in the next chapter, but the effect that it has had on the CSA's Australian counterpart is equally impressive.

Consider the costs that are accumulated by the CSA at present. Under the current system two parents may fight for custody of their child, one will win and be deemed the resident parent; one will lose and be deemed the absent parent. The absent parent is then required to pay the resident parent an amount of money, which the CSA is often involved in determining and collecting. To do this they need staff. The Child Maintenance and Enforcement Commission is not short on staff, although *"the Commission has reduced staff numbers (full-time equivalents) from a peak of 11,386 in 2006-07 to 8,251 in 2010-11"*[53]. This first overhead, then, will cost CMES the salaries of those staff, desk space, the cost of initial and ongoing training etc. In the U.K. there are so many cases of divorce and so many disputes over custody that the agency needs to get involved in an incredible number. So they need more staff. They then find that some parents dispute the rulings so much that they will not engage with the agency (see the F4J quote above). So then they have to hire investigators to work for them adding more cost to the agency. The arrears bill builds up (currently at £3.8bn) so they hire more staff to help clear the backlog and invest in a half-a-billion pound computer and telephone system to streamline the workload. It goes on.

Following the Australian model there is a presumption of shared custody. There is no resident parent as a necessity, there is no absent parent as a necessity. Therefore there cannot be a payment made by the absent parent to resident parent and the only way a transfer of funds can take place is based on time spent with the children. If, however, there is a presumption of *equal* custody then, if the normal course of events are allowed to follow, neither parents will have (significantly) more time with the children so there will be no net transfer of funds, no dispute over contact and no reason for the CSA to get involved.

If the parents agree that, say, one works longer hours and therefore should spend less time with the child then there may be a requirement for a support payment to be made. However, the key term here is *'agree'*. Because parents have come to their own arrangements rather than taking to the gladiatorial arena that is the family court system and subsequently having their arrangements forced upon them, they are likely to agree on the outcome, particularly if there are some pre-written guidelines related to what should be paid in what circumstances (for example, for every day more a child spends with one parent rather than the other, the other should pay X percentage of their earnings to the one).

The only *raison d'être* for the CSA in these circumstances would be to search for, enforce payments from and if necessary prosecute recalcitrant parents. Therefore they could save on the cost of staff, premises, computers etc. and make the sort of economies observed in Australia. It would also give the agency more time to deal with some of the issues that face them today, with which they are currently overwhelmed, and which lead to *"poor customer service, inefficient processing of cases and inaccurate calculations"*[54]. We can already see evidence that reducing the CSA's workload can improve its effectiveness and ability to concentrate on its essential purpose. As the government website states:

"The repeal of Section 6 of the Child Support Act 1991 by the Child Maintenance and Other Payments Act 2008 removed the compulsion for parents with main day-to-day care in receipt of out-of-work benefits to apply for statutory child

maintenance. This compulsion was removed for parents newly claiming benefits from July 2008 and for existing claimants from October 2008. In March 2008, the Agency received 34,700 applications; this number had fallen to 8,200 in March 2009."[54]

In other words to claim benefits a resident parent was no longer required by law to request maintenance payments through the CSA. The resultant decline in applications meant that the CSA drastically improved its performance:

- *"In 2005-06, 423,000 of the 5.3 million telephone calls made to the CSA were abandoned by the customer waiting to speak to a member of staff. The average time taken to answer a call from the queue stood at 59 seconds...around 52,000 calls were abandoned during 2008-09 out of a similar volume of calls [when the average time taken to answer a call was 13 seconds]"*
- *"The percentage of current scheme applications cleared within 12 weeks increased from 52% [in February 2006] to 81% in March 2009*
- *"In April 2006...the backlog stood at 282,400 cases waiting to be cleared by the CSA...[in March 2009] the number of uncleared current scheme cases had fallen to 49,400 and there were 6,800 uncleared old scheme cases"*

It can only be imagined what sort of service the CSA could provide if they were removed of the burden of having to involve themselves in the volume of cases that they currently do. The quote at the start of the chapter is from the DWP acknowledging, in a reactionary sort of way, the need to reduce the burden on the CSA. It is a positive move, though, in more ways than one. Any action (or rather in this case a conscious decision not to act) that promotes parents achieving their own agreements and thereby removing unnecessary conflict is a good thing for all involved. In reality the way that things are moving is such that the role of the CSA is being reigned in, and potentially in future the government will acknowledge that the state should only be involved in enforcement in cases where it absolutely has to be. Rather than being involved in hundreds of thousands of cases where it is not really needed and, consequently, providing a poorer service to everyone, a future Child Maintenance Group can be a specialist unit doing essential work with disengaged parents. So by encouraging separated parties to come to their own agreements, the state can provide a better service to those it does encounter, whilst keeping out of the lives of those it doesn't need to be involved it.

Reforming family law would have the benefit of aiding all of these positives. It would also create greater fairness in child support because if both parents are allowed to split their time equally, and therefore there is no net transfer of funds from one parent to the other, there can be no dispute over child support (no parents can claim that they pay more than other in similar circumstances or that they are being made to pay cash for the impairment of not being able to spend time with their children).

In other words changing family law in line with the Baker plan would benefit the CSA, the people who come into contact with the CSA (claimant parents in the form of speed of processing claims) and the taxpayer (reduced costs of enforcement with the CSA currently spending more than one-and-a-half times on costs what its Australian counterpart does, where reform has already been introduced).

So far we have seen that changing family law would be fairer to fathers, of benefit to women in general and single mothers in particular, of benefit to industry and the economy and would ease the role of the CSA. However, although all these factors are worthy of consideration, the paramountcy principle states that none of them are of overriding concern, if the welfare of the children would be affected negatively in the face of change. Therefore no assessment of the case for change can be complete without an evaluation of this, most important of consequences.

What About the Children?
The paramount consideration

*"Fundamentally, this is not about the rights of the parents,
it's about the welfare of the children and we should be
focused entirely on that"*

-   David Norgrove, Chairman of Family Justice Review,
    3rd November 2011

Effectively this entire book, when investigating the impact of reforming the law on all the people and institutions that would subsequently be affected, has had running throughout it the conflict between two opposing arguments. Firstly there is the side reflected by the current law in the U.K:

Shared parenting cannot work in practice (chapter two and chapter five)
It is unfair to expect a child to live in two homes (chapter one and chapter five)
Separated parents are too contentious to share custody (chapter one)
Regular contact is sufficient involvement (chapter one)
Shared parenting means that children suffer because child support payments decrease (chapter six)

Next there is the model recently favoured by nations such as Australia and, to a lesser extent, Germany, Canada and certain states within the U.S.A.:

Shared parenting can lead to more fulfilling lives for both parents as well as the child, particularly where the child previously enjoyed relationships with two involved parents (chapter two and chapter five)

It is unfair to expect a child to forfeit part of their relationship with one parent (chapter one, chapter two, chapter five and chapter six)

Non-resident parents suffer when contact orders are not adhered to (chapter two)

Regular contact is a poor substitute for the relationship that the non-resident parent and child would have enjoyed before the separation (chapter one)

Shared parenting means that both parents directly pay for the child, rather than paying each other, meaning that the children benefit (chapter six)

Really, though, these conflicting issues need greater exploration in the context of their actual effects on the children involved. Norgrove's comment at the start of this chapter, which simply reflects the paramountcy principle already discussed, is absolutely correct; the best interests of the child should be the ultimate consideration of any decision made in relation to the law in this area. So Norgrove stated that he is determined to focus on *"the welfare of the children"*, but what does this mean? Is it as black-and-white as that the status quo acknowledges the welfare of the children in custody cases whereas reforming the law would not? The only case study we can really use from recent times is that of Australia, which had laws similar to that of the U.K. at the turn of the millennium and then amended the law to a presumption of shared custody in 2006. Significantly, immediately following the passing of the Family Law

Amendment (Shared Parental Responsibility) Act 2006, The Family Court of Australia had cause to comment on the new laws in one of their earlier rulings. In the case of *Goode & Goode [2006] Fam CA 1346*, The Family Court of Australia acknowledged that the effects of the Act meant that shared time should always be the presumption of the court when making an order and that *"the child's best interests remain the overriding consideration."*[55]

Claiming that they can presume shared custody for both parents whilst still professing to act in the best interests of the child flies in the face of everything that proponents of the status quo in the U.K. claim as irrefutable. This at least demonstrates that the arguments that children are better off with one home than with two involved parents are inconclusive, certainly not absolute as Norgrove's FJR and others would claim. So there are two schools of thought to be considered, purely in the context of the effects on the children, and that is what the rest of this chapter is dedicated to.

The first school of thought is reflected in the status quo; children need one stable home and therefore the non-resident parent should be entitled to 'contact' with the child, but not joint (and certainly not equal) residence. The rationale behind this is that children will benefit, both psychologically and emotionally, from this approach and that no change should be considered unless it can be proved that this is not the case. In a shared residence situation, children effectively have two homes rather than one. The dilution of a 'permanent base' that is caused by this shift means that a child will never really know where he or she belongs, the consequences of which are that they may grow up confused and poorly adjusted. Liz Trinder, a professor of law at the University of

Exeter, has argued vehemently in favour of maintaining the present principles of family law, claiming that any deviation into shared care options would reduce the focus on the paramountcy principle. In order to demonstrate that there is no benefit to shared care she stressed that during her study she found that *"children with more contact were doing no better or worse than children with less contact"*[56]. Trinder used this evidence to further her argument that there should be no change to the law as children would be no better off. What she perhaps failed to recognise, and what should certainly be highlighted, is that her evidence, if it is as sound as she professes, demonstrates that children in shared care are no worse off than children in primary-care households.

Two years after publishing her thesis, Trinder wrote an article in *The Guardian* in response to the FJR in which she argued that there is no need for legislation to promote shared parenting as most parents have access to their children anyway. In fact in terms of contact order applications *"in 2010 the courts refused only 300 of 95,000"*[57]. Those 300 rejected applications may well be the result of a court's concern regarding domestic abuse, so if all other contact applications are granted, surely there is no requirement for a change in the law? The problem is that here Trinder is misleading her audience. She states that there is no requirement to change the law to favour shared custody as a right, because applications for contact are already granted by the courts. However, contact is not the same as residence, as we have already seen. A residence order is granted by the court and it determines who children will live with. A contact order, also granted by the family courts, simply grants a parent a set period of time each week during which they may see their children. A parent who has been declined the right to shared residence will then be labelled the 'absent parent' and subsequently forced to make an application to a court asking for permission to see their children. The court will then normally grant this request and allot that parent an amount of time (for example, every-other weekend). Most applicants for contact orders find the process insulting and humiliating, whilst not being satisfied with the outcome but they make the application due to having no other option in terms of access.

In her initial report Trinder did concede that *"compared to more traditional primary carer arrangements, shared care parents are more likely to communicate more often and more likely to share in decision making."*[58] However, she also provides the final argument in terms of keeping the law as it is, and that is the continuation of arrangements. She asserted that in Australia, where the law was changed in favour of shared care several years ago, *"only 49% of shared time arrangements were still in place after 4-5 years, compared to 87% of primary mother care arrangements."*[59]

There are two distinct points which must be drawn from this final argument. The first is that many people will look at that statistic as a good thing. Around half of parents are maintaining shared residence after five years and the half that aren't have therefore made their own arrangements to suit themselves and their children. That is surely much better than having an order imposed on them that at least one, and probably both, parents are unhappy with. Arrangements are bound to be tweaked and amended according to children's and parents' changing lives (if one parent changes jobs, when children go to school, if children partake in extra-curricular activities etc., these all have to be accounted for). Trinder's definition of shared residence is where each parent has time with their children between 35%-65% of the time. If they fall slightly out of this bracket due to them being flexible and amending their schedules to accommodate all of the parties involved, then this should be celebrated. As Trinder herself said, *"shared care parents are more likely to communicate more often and more likely to share in decision making"*. Anything that removes the causes of conflict following a separation should be examined further.

The second point to be taken from Trinder's arguments about continuity is that by ambiguously stating that *"only 49% of arrangements are still in place"* there is no examination into which way the 51% reverted. That is to say, at the moment there is an overwhelming skew in favour of single mothers, over single fathers, when residence is awarded. Once joint residence is awarded neither parent is deemed to be the secondary carer. Therefore when they rework their own arrangements to make them more suitable for themselves and for their children, there is nothing to suggest that the balance of care is not sometimes weighted towards the father. In reality it matters not which parents it ends up weighted towards, but if the balance was closer to 50%-50% father-mother, than the current 7%-93% father-mother, then there could be no accusations of bias.

This brings us neatly on to one, less considered, argument. Before evaluating the case for shared residence, there is still one argument in favour of keeping the primary-carer system that is currently in place, whilst simultaneously making it fairer. Those who subscribe to the arguments above (that children are more balanced and have greater stability in the current system, that most contact orders are granted anyway and that change would lead to a lack of continuity in arrangements) are still unable to reconcile the claims of people such as Liz Trinder who argue that *"the claim of systematic bias against fathers is a myth"* with the fact that, as we discovered in the prologue, 93% of single parent families are headed by a single mother. It could just be a coincidence that when two parents go to court to argue over residence the court just happens to come down in favour of the mother…in almost every case…for 24 years. Or else there could be some genuine underlying sub-conscious prejudice there in which judges, suffering the same upbringing and social encounters as the employers of chapter 5, the opponents of feminism in chapter 4 and the politicians in chapter 3, see women as carers and men as not.

If we do subscribe to the arguments above, and we are convinced that children need one stable home, not two involved parents, and we are not biased against anybody on the basis of their gender, then there is no reason that 50% of single parent households should be headed by women, 50% by men. With this in mind, proponents of the status quo should argue in favour of courts keeping statistics of cases where they award residence in favour of the woman and cases where they award residence in favour of the man and ensure that they are working at a target of 50% at all times. There would have to be no good reason for awarding in favour of one parent instead of the other, but then there doesn't seem to be at present either. (Perhaps to begin with, much in the manner of positive discrimination employed in the workplace to promote the numbers of females in higher positions, there could be a presumption in favour of men, just to get the balance right?). The consequences of this would be as follows:

More men would become primary carers, there would be greater equality amongst the sexes after court cases so justice could be said to be satisfied.

More women would be free to commit to working careers rather than caring, so they would go further in the workplace.

Both mothers and fathers would be paying child support in roughly equal numbers, so child maintenance cannot be deemed to be prejudiced.

Children would still have one stable home so they would not be affected in the slightest.

In reality, conflict would reduce. The absolute uncertainty of the outcome for parents would mean that they are less likely to litigate because the chances of them losing custody of their children, regardless of their gender, is 50%. Rather than risk this, both parents will likely wish to negotiate something that works for them, or go to arbitration to settle it rather than fighting in court.

The alternative arguments are in favour of reforming the system so that there is a presumption of shared custody. Initially, there are the counter-arguments to those made above. The first of these relates to the instability which may be caused by having two homes. There is a good deal of research which has gone into this issue and many have found that instability is often confused with a lack of predictability. If a child knows in advance their own routines they are not forsaking stability. D. A. Luepnitz produced a study in the 1980s showing that children seemed happy with their exposure to both parents, whereas children in single-parent families were dissatisfied with the amount of time they saw the non-resident parent.[60]

The present system is unnecessarily adversarial, it polarises parents by forcing them to fight in court for time with their children and this has terrible consequences for the children involved. A system which created certainty (for example, each parent will share time with their children) would limit the need for court battles and therefore produce a more harmonious relationship between parents.

The strongest negative effect on children of the current system, though, is the effect that fatherlessness has on their psyche. There have been studies that show that children headed by single-parent families suffer more with issues of self-hate and depression than those in joint residence families. This may eventually manifest itself as criminality in the most violent possible way. In his essay 'Gangs and the Curse of Fatherlessness', Gordon Dalbey, a commentator from the U.S.A. wrote about how young boys turn to gangs because of a lack of a male role model at home. He quoted mothers as saying:

"I don't understand why he goes out on the streets...I'm a good mother. I keep a clean house, I go to church, I don't run around with men, I cook for the boy, wash his clothes, and provide a good home. Why doesn't he want to stay here?"[61]

He concluded that no matter how good a mother a woman may be, *"a boy is drawn to the gang by the innate male longing and need to break away from the mother, bond to the father, and be joined thereby to the company of men"*.

In August 2011 the most major cities in the U.K. were besieged by rioters; gangs of young people causing violence, damage and looting. There were many possible reasons put forward as to why young people could behave in this way.

Looting? Perhaps they desperately wanted a new pair of trainers. That doesn't really explain the violence, unnecessary damage and arson, though. These were gangs of people, who spent nights in the company of other young people out on the streets, rather than at home with their parents. The reason for the riots was a gang culture developing in all major cities across the U.K., and the reason for gangs is clear. David Lammy, Labour MP for Tottenham where the rioting started in 2011 stated decisively that *"we are seeing huge consequences of the lack of male role models in young men's lives"*[62].

On the other side of the political divide, Conservative minister Iain Duncan Smith took a similar view, stating that *"many young gang members drift in from dysfunctional broken backgrounds in search of a place to belong, a perverse kind of family...with no role models except the violent and the criminal"*[63].

Journalist Melanie Phillips agreed: *"of course there are many lone parents who do a tremendous job. But we're talking about widespread social collapse. And there are whole areas of Britain, white as well as black, where committed fathers are a wholly unknown phenomenon"*.

The Bishop of London commented that the *"background to the riots is family breakdown and the absence of strong and positive role models"*.

When all political parties agree, and are supported by both the media and the Church, then they must certainly have identified the correct diagnosis for the country's ills. Therefore it seems as though the position taken by all parties involved in family law actually leads to the formation of gang culture within the U.K. In fact, even without the gang element, children who grow up without a father around for significant periods of time tend to suffer more than average from delinquency, aggression and disobedience, according to studies by the University of Pittsburg.[64]

Finally, children who have one parent removed from their lives tend to suffer from abandonment issues, often even interpreting the split and sudden loss of contact with that parent as their fault. Children who experience this often develop slower and to a lesser extent than their peers, and eventually the experience will manifest itself in adulthood in a number of ways:

- Avoiding close relationships and friendships. Children who have internalised their feelings of abandonment go on to use the experience as part of their self-preservation in future years. Everybody subconsciously uses their past experiences to determine how they react to present events; if something has worked well in the past it will be repeated, if behaviour has worked badly it will be discarded. Children who have a close relationship with a parent and then have that parent removed from their lives feel the pain of the separation as much as either of the other parties involved. They then learn from that not to let people get close to them again, so as to avoid that pain. They may become unable to trust others, their concept of protecting their 'self' preventing them to allow others to become close. They have to control their own world, and letting themselves open to other people emotionally removes some of that control.
- Difficulty with intimacy and closeness. For similar reasons to the above. They may have difficulty building a rapport with their peers and are usually unable to share their feelings with friends or partners not least because

they don't always (allow themselves to) feel the same emotions as everybody else.

- More likely to engage in casual sex. This stems from their need to control; people with abandonment issues such as avoidant attachment disorder cannot be open with other people in the same way that someone who hasn't suffered abandonment may, so sex may not be associated with love in the same way is it is for others. In these cases, sex is often used either as a means to be liked (another person may like them if they have sex with them, and this leaves the sufferer feeling less vulnerable than asking to be liked) or as a perverse means of feeling a closeness that they are otherwise too fearful to commit to.

We can see here that there is nothing to suggest that keeping the law as it is benefits children, but much to suggest, albeit with only a limited amount of research, that changing the law could be of great benefit to the children of divorce. Does this alone not make it worth trying? If the current system does not work, does not provide fairness, equality or justice, is not efficient, creates drawn-out and highly emotional contests, directly leads to the subjugation of women in industry, is a drain on the economy and may well be leading to a generation of emotionally-challenged children, then how can we justify not considering a change.

Throughout this book the underlying assumption has been that the welfare of the children should be the paramount consideration of any decision made within family law, whether by a judge in an individual case or by the legislative in changing the law. Not surprisingly, this is the one principle on which all the major players involved agree:

The Family Justice Review stated that they should be *"focused entirely"* on *"the welfare of the children"*.

Dame Butler-Sloss claims that as far as the courts are concerned *"the welfare of the children is the first and paramount consideration"*.

The government also state that *"the welfare needs of the child are the paramount consideration...this remains the 'gold standard.'"*[65]

Parenting website mumsnet concurs: [the] *"paramount consideration is the child's welfare"* (tellingly, they also acknowledge that *"individual judges may have personal attitudes (or prejudices) regarding...caring roles and abilities"*[66]).

F4J actively promote this: *"the rights of children are paramount"* and *"you cannot separate a child's right from its parents' rights"*.

The welfare of children should be of paramount consideration, yet on the basis of the evidence we have seen, it isn't. If the paramountcy principle is to be realised, then change is required; the blueprint is there in the form of F4J's ten point plan, or FNF's five point strategy. The system can take the form of changes made in Australia or North America. The West is slowly, too slowly, though I would argue inexorably moving towards shared residence as the benefits are becoming realised. If we are to promote the welfare of the generations to come – the mental health and the emotional health – then we need to start with reforming family law.

Epilogue
The Future

"By abolishing the uncivilised battle for possession of a child by two people who once loved each other, the Children Bill, which emphasizes the importance of both mothers and fathers in child-rearing, will end the inhuman, callous and cruel practice of divorcing a child from one of his or her loyal and devoted parents"

- Ray Powell MP, Commons Speech, 27th April 2019* (second reading of the Children Bill which will end discrimination in family law)

*accurate quote, inaccurate date

I flatter David Charter by presenting this epilogue in a format similar to his final chapter of *Au Revoir, Europe*, in which this ultimate section was presented as a fictional future based on the assumptions made in previous chapters. But it was so splendidly done that I felt it had to be mimicked, so here goes.

The year is 2019 and the U.K. is four years into its second ever fixed term Parliament. On the floor of the House of Commons Members of Parliament are discussing the second Children Bill, presented thirty years after the first and designed to correct what has become seen as some injustices within the current system, following extensive research into the working practices of the family courts. The Bill is currently at its second reading, having originated in the House of Lords, and members are to vote on it later in the evening, after which it is expected to pass through to committee stage.

The Bill proposes amongst other things that there will be a presumption of 50/50 starting point for custody of a child in cases of separation; that even where parents agree that this cannot work in their circumstances children have a right to a 'meaningful relationship' with both parents; and that the verdicts passed by judges should be monitored so that the judiciary may be held to account for their decisions. The Labour MP for Ogmore, Ray Powell, has just stood and given a speech in the chamber, quoted at the start of the chapter. In it he praised the emphasis placed on the importance of the role of both parents within the Bill and the end of forcibly separating a child *"from one of his or her loyal and devoted parents"*. The speech was followed by chants of *"hear, hear!"* around the chamber. Few representatives present disagree that removing a child from its parents is *"inhuman, callous and cruel"*. He followed on from the above quote to assert that he found it *"heart-breaking"* to meet with constituents who are going through a divorce, knowing that if they cannot reach an agreement the state will forcibly remove the children from one of the parents. Thank God for this Bill. He went on to express his regret that the Bill does not legislate for the rights of grandparents:

"I have received thousands of letters from grandparents all over the country which I have read and re-read...grandparents who find themselves deprived of the opportunity to be with and to love their grandchildren, or even to see them...When grandparents have to hide behind church walls, bus shelters, school walls and school toilets just to get a glimpse of their grandchildren, there is something wrong with the law...in today's society, where everybody is on the grab for what they can get, grandparents are only

offering their love to someone else. They do not want anything from their grandchildren – all that they want is to give something. It is a refreshing change in today's avaricious society to have people who want to give something instead of always wanting to take."

However, Rome was not built in a day and sometimes, with law, we have to accept that change happens incrementally. It was an emotive speech, and was followed by others on both sides of the House who pledged support for the Bill and its prompt acceptance through committee stage. The feeling was that this piece of legislation was long overdue, but at least it was here now. Surely, if the members of the House of Commons are so convinced that they are casting votes to end the practice of divorcing children from their parents, then this is the outcome that will occur?

Actually, no.

The asterisk at the beginning of the chapter states that this was an accurate quote from Mr Powell, with an inaccurate date. This was actually an excerpt from a speech that the late Sir Ray Powell gave in the House of Commons at the second reading of the first Children Bill, which would later become The Children Act, in 1989. The Bill promised to end the separation of parents from their children because of the injustice of it up until that point. Those reading it were convinced that it acknowledged the role of both parents and that by passing this legislation, there would be greater justice for all and a more fulfilling life for the children. Few people at the time considered the enormous power over interpretation of the legislation that judges would be entrusted with in the future. For example, TCA appears to recognise both parents, and it appears to make a sensible assertion with the inclusion of the paramountcy principle, which at the time was just one line inserted into the Act that was easily overlooked. However, the consequences of this were enormous. For the quarter of a century that has followed judges, guided by a belief that children are better off with one home than with two involved parents, which is not written in legislation, have been able to use the paramountcy principle as a means to enforce this prejudice in favour of those they see as carers; mothers. This has come at the expense of fathers. *"Heart-breaking"* expense.

Written into TCA is what appears to be another fairly innocent statement, which was quoted at the start of chapter one and which was followed shortly afterwards by a promise, as of yet unfulfilled, to explore it in more detail. This was a quote on www.gov.uk that *"all mothers and most fathers have legal rights and responsibilities as parents"*, which stems from Section 2 of TCA (a mother automatically has parental responsibility for her child but a father does not necessarily, unless he is married to the mother). If nothing else is settled upon in this book (and those for and against change are equally vehement in their position and unlikely to back down, so it may not be) then this one issue should be: that *no* mothers and *no* fathers should ever be denied rights and responsibilities to their children, therefore *all* mothers and *all* fathers should have legal rights and responsibilities, regardless of how the state then interprets their respective roles.

The argument for stating that all mothers have rights is that they are the only person guaranteed to be present at the birth of the child. If they then disappear from the scene then that is a tragedy, but they never relinquish their rights or indeed their responsibilities. Fathers, on the other hand, may not be known or may not be added to the birth certificate etc. Frankly, there is no evidence whatsoever that this should change anything. Those same fathers should still be entitled to the same rights and responsibilities as the mother; in nature they do, but this is not reflected in a law which brands them as inferior based on their gender. If a father disappears before the birth of the child and cannot be traced or the mother is unable or unwilling to name the father, then these are issues which should be dealt with in a different manner and entirely separately. The fact is that there is a father and that father should be entitled to the same rights as any other parent.

References

Prologue

1. www.barcouncil.org/media-centre/news-and-press-releases/2013/june/bar-council-responds-to-legal-aid-consultation
2. https://www.gov.uk/government/uploads/system/uploads/attachment_data/file/162303/fjr-exec-summary.pdf.pdf
3. http://www.dailymail.co.uk/news/article-2056375/Fathers-lose-bid-equal-custody-rights-review-family-law.html

A Piecemeal Approach

4. Section 1 The Children Act 1989, Hansard, referenced from www.legislation.gov, June 2013
5. http://news.bbc.co.uk/1/hi/uk_politics/3995505.stm
6. http://www.fnf.org.uk/news-and-events/press-releases/2004-archive/041110
7. Elster, J., 1987, *Solomonic Judgments; Against The Best Interests of the Child*, University of Chicago Law Review, p.40-53

Pragmatism or Justice?

8. *Family Justice Review Final Report*, November 2011
9. Lord Wright quoted in Martin, J., 2002, p.11, *The English Legal System, 3rd Edition*, Hodder & Stoughton, Berwick upon Tweed
10. Rawls, J., 1973, *A Theory of Justice*, Oxford, Oxford University Press, p.504

11. Ibid, p.11

12. Rogers, B., 1999, 'Portrait, John Rawls', *Prospect*, issue 42, p.51

13. Family Justice Council in *Family Justice Review Final Report*, November 2011, p.141

14. http://www.dailymail.co.uk/news/article-2056375/Fathers-lose-bid-equal-custody-rights-review-family-law.html

15. *Family Justice Review Final Report*, November 2011, p.41

16. Ministry of Justice, 2013, *Court Statistics Quarterly October to December 2012*, Ministry of Justice Statistics Bulletin

17. http://www.humanrightsaction.org/vaeter/shared-custody.html

18. http://www.familylawweek.co.uk/site.aspx?i=ed57393

19. http://www.fathers-4-justice.org/our-campaign/our-10-point-blueprint-for-family-law/

20. http://www.legislation.gov.uk/ukpga/1998/42/schedule/1/part/I/chapter/7

21. Rawls, J., quoted in Rogers, B., 1999, 'Portrait John Rawls', *Prospect*, issue 42, p.50

Political Suicide

22. http://romsey.conservativesintouch.com/news/216/

23. Thatcher, M., 1993, *The Downing Street Years*, p.281, Harper Collins, London

24. Duncan Smith, I., 'Together We Can Beat The Gangs', *The Guardian*, 18th August 2011

25. Heywood, A., 2007, *Politics Third Edition*, p.267

26. Wheatcroft, G. 2005, *The Strange Death of Tory England*, p.34, Penguin Books, London
27. De Tocqueville, A., quoted in Heywood, A., 2007, *Politics Third Edition*, p.271, Palgrave Macmillan, Basingstoke
28. Burke, E., 1790, *Reflections on the French Revolution,* paragraph 403
29. http://www.reuters.com/article/2010/11/09/us-bush-book-oprah-idUSTRE6A840J20101109

Living with an Equal

30. http://www.guardian.co.uk/commentisfree/2013/apr/11/every-woman-boardroom-pull-more-up
31. http://www.thesun.co.uk/sol/homepage/news/4967300/Queens-portrait-is-defaced-by-spray-painting-vandals.html
32. Mill, J.S., 1869, 'The subjection of women', in Mill, J.S., (1975)*Three Essays*, Oxford, Oxford University Press, p.485
33. Tronto, J.C., 1993, *Moral Boundaries: A Political Argument for an Ethic of Care*, New York and London, Routledge, p.174-175
34. http://www.mirror.co.uk/money/personal-finance/tuc-study-women-losing-out-1449166
35. http://talentreadiness.wordpress.com/2008/06/23/demographic-trends-the-uk-workforcebrewing-risks/
36. http://www.parentdish.co.uk/2012/03/14/universal-credit-why-150-000-single-working-mums-will-be-worse-off/

37. Office for National Statistics, *Annual Survey of Hours and Earnings, 2012, Provisional Results*, 22 November 2012, p.7

De-industrial Revolution

38. Chartered Institute of Personnel & Development, 2013, *Megatrends: The Trends Shaping Work and Working Lives*, p.3/p.12
39. http://www.debtbombshell.com/public-spending.htm
40. www.gov.uk/flexible-working/overview
41. Chartered Institute of Personnel & Development, 2013, *Megatrends: The Trends Shaping Work and Working Lives*, p.12
42. Lindsay, C., March 2003, *A Century of Labour Market Change*, Office for National Statistics
43. Thompson, J. and Truch, E., *The Flex Factor, Realising the value of flexible working*, RSA Action and Research Centre, July 2013
44. http://www.theguardian.com/news/datablog/2013/jan/ 08/uk-benefit-welfare-spending#zoomed-picture
45. Department for Work and Pensions, *Benefit and Tax Credit expenditure in Great Britain*, January 2013, p.6
46. www.fathers-4-justice.org/about-f4j/fact-sheet/
47. The Centre for Social Justice, *Child Benefit Reform: Dealing with the Deficits to put Stable Families First*, March 2012

'Tax on Fatherhood'

48. Department for Work and Pensions, 2012, *Supporting Separated Families; Securing Children's Futures*, London

49. http://www.theguardian.com/society/2006/feb/09/childrensservices.politics

50. http://www.independent.co.uk/voices/when-protest-turns-to-poison-lies-intimidation-and-thuggery-are-marring-the-campaign-against-the-csa-as-yasmin-alibhaibrown-discovered-1423840.html

51. http://www.fathers-4-justice.org/about-f4j/campaign-faqs/

52. House of Commons Committee of Public Accounts, 18 May 2012, *Child Maintenance and Enforcement Commission: Cost Reductions*, Eighty-third Report of Session 2010-12, London, The Stationary Office Ltd

53. National Audit Office, 29 February 2012, *Child Maintenance and Enforcement Commission: Cost Reductions*, Report by the Comptroller and Auditor General, HC 1793, London

54. http://www.publications.parliament.uk/pa/cm200910/cmselect/cmworpen/118/11806.htm

What About the Children?

55. http://www.international-divorce.com/australia_child_custody.htm

56. Trinder, L., Shared residence: a review of recent research evidence, p.490 *Child and Family Law Quarterly, Vol 22, No 4, 2010*

57. http://www.theguardian.com/commentisfree/2012/feb/06/no-bias-against-fathers-childrens-act

58. Trinder, L., Shared residence: a review of recent research evidence, p.481 *Child and Family Law Quarterly, Vol 22, No 4,* 2010

59. Ibid, p.484

60. Luepnitz, D. A., 1982, *Child Custody: A Study of Families After Divorce,* Lexington Books

61. Dalbey, G., 25/03/2007, Gangs and the Curse of Fatherlessness, *Santa Barbara News Press*, Santa Barbara, California

62. http://www.christian.org.uk/news/riots-where-are-the-fathers/

63. http://www.theguardian.com/politics/2011/oct/03/duncan-smith-riots-benefits-system

64. http://www.pitt.edu/ppcl/Publications/chapters/children_of_divorce.htm

65. Ministry of Justice/Department for Education, February 2012, *The Government Response to the Family Justice Review: A system with children and families at its heart,* p.20

66. http://www.mumsnet.com/divorce-and-separation/child-contact-faqs

Epilogue
All quotes sourced from Hansard 27/04/1989:
www.publications.parliament.uk/pa/cm198889/cmhansrd/1989-04-27/Debate-4.html

Index

Please keep an eye out for *The Tories* by Adam Wordsworth. Coming soon.

To contact the author please get in touch with Springlands Press using the contact details below.

Enquiries
Springlands Press Ltd,
10 Broad Birches,
Ellesmere Port,
Cheshire,
CH65 3AB

Or alternatively fill out an enquiry form via our website:
www.springlandspublishing.co.uk

DADS
UNDER
PRESSURE